An Inner World

An Inner World

Seventeenth-Century Dutch Genre Painting

EDITED BY
Heather Moqtaderi and Lara Yeager-Crasselt

WITH ESSAYS BY
Shira Brisman
Eric Jorink
Lara Yeager-Crasselt

ADDITIONAL CONTRIBUTIONS BY
Caroline Van Cauwenberge

Arthur Ross Gallery, University of Pennsylvania, Philadelphia

Distributed by the University of Pennsylvania Press

Published on the occasion of the exhibition *An Inner World: Seventeenth-Century Dutch Genre Painting* at the Arthur Ross Gallery, co-curated by Lara Yeager-Crasselt, curator of The Leiden Collection, and Heather Moqtaderi, assistant director and curator of the Arthur Ross Gallery, on view April 17–July 25, 2021.

Support from the Netherland-America Foundation and the David J. Evans Exhibition Fund made this catalogue possible. The related exhibition was made possible through the generous sponsorship of David J. Evans III (WG'70) through the David J. Evans Exhibition Fund. Additional support for the exhibition at the Arthur Ross Gallery is provided by the J & AR Foundation, Bill and Kathie Hohns, and the Patron's Circle.

FRONT COVER: Gabriel Metsu, *Woman Reading a Book by a Window*, ca. 1653–54, detail, oil on canvas, 41 $^{5}/_{16}$ × 35 ¾ in. (105 × 90.7 cm). The Leiden Collection, New York.

BACK COVER: Cesare Ripa, *Cognizione*, engraving, 4 ¾ × 3 $^{9}/_{16}$ in. (12 × 8.8 cm), in Cesare Ripa, *Iconologia de cavaliere Cesare Ripa, Perugino* (*Iconologia [or Moral Emblems], of the Cavalier Cesare Ripa, Perugia*), volume 2 (Perugia: Piergiovanni Costantini, 1764–67), 69. Kislak Center for Special Collections, Rare Books, and Manuscripts, University of Pennsylvania, Philadelphia.

INSIDE BACK COVER: Embroidered book binding, 6 $^{3}/_{16}$ × 3 ¾ × 2 $^{9}/_{16}$ in. (15.7 × 9.5 × 6.5 cm), Paulus van Ravesteÿn, *Dat is Biblia. De gantsche H. Schrifture* (*The Entire Holy Scripture*) (Amsterdam: Paulus van Ravesteÿn, 1657). Kislak Center for Special Collections, Rare Books, and Manuscripts, University of Pennsylvania, Philadelphia.

PHOTOGRAPHY CREDITS
Pages 6, 10, 12, 18, 34, 35, 53, 58, 68, 72: Courtesy of The Leiden Collection, New York

Fig. 2.3: Photo by Paul Litherland

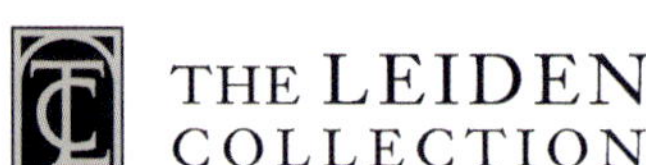

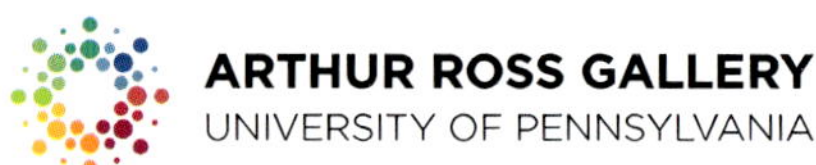

Contents

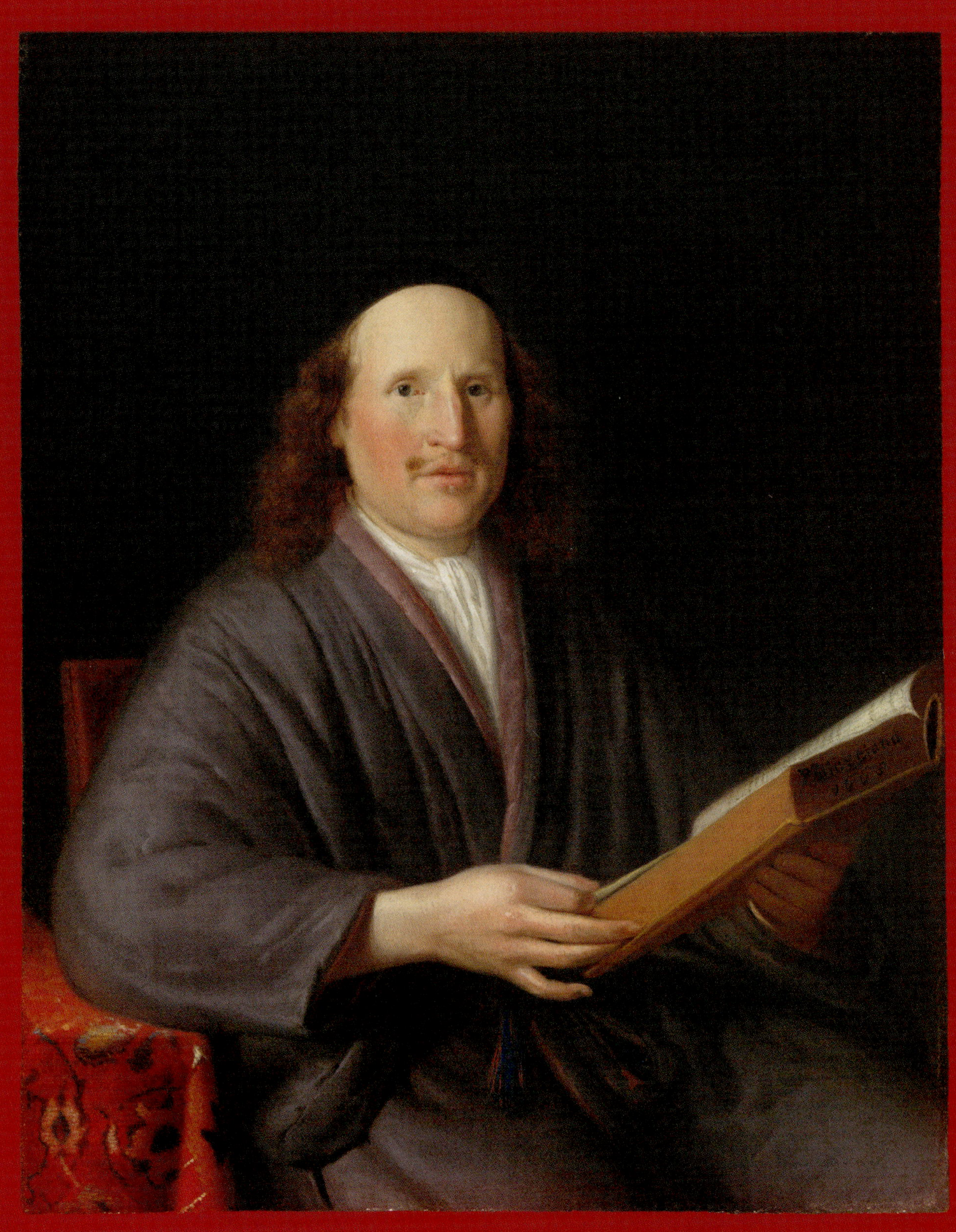

The Arthur Ross Gallery is proud to present *An Inner World: Seventeenth-Century Dutch Genre Painting*. The exquisite paintings presented in this exhibition were executed by artists working in or near the city of Leiden in the Dutch Golden Age. In addition, a selection of seventeenth-century rare books enlighten and expand the intellectual context of these paintings. In the mid-1600s, Leiden was renowned for its university, for its *fijnschilders* (fine painters), for its textiles, and as a center of Dutch Protestant life. A centerpiece of this exhibition, Gabriel Metsu's *Woman Reading by a Window* (cat. 4), depicts a woman sitting quietly in a domestic interior, gazing at an open book in deep reflection. The painting reveals the artist's close observation not only of nature but also of the life of the mind, both important values affirmed at Leiden University.

An Inner World is co-curated by Lara Yeager-Crasselt, curator of The Leiden Collection, New York, and Heather Moqtaderi, assistant director and curator of the Arthur Ross Gallery at the University of Pennsylvania. This is an expanded version of an exhibition Yeager-Crasselt first organized for the Sterling and Francine Clark Art Institute, in Williamstown, Massachusetts, in 2017.

I am deeply grateful to Thomas S. Kaplan and Daphne Recanati Kaplan for their generosity in lending nine paintings from The Leiden Collection for this exhibition. I would also like to thank Olivier Meslay, Hardymon Director of the Clark Art Institute, for an important loan from the Clark's collection. I would like to extend special thanks to our colleagues at the Kislak Center for Special Collections, Rare Books, and Manuscripts at the University of Pennsylvania for lending a selection of rare books from their collection of seventeenth-century literature. The three essays in this catalogue present new scholarship by Lara Yeager-Crasselt as well as Shira Brisman, assistant professor of the history of art at the University of Pennsylvania, and Eric Jorink, Teylers Professor of Enlightenment and Religion at Leiden University. I thank them, along with Heather Moqtaderi and Caroline Van Cauwenberge, curatorial associate and digital content coordinator at The Leiden Collection, for their important contributions to the publication, which greatly enhances this exceptional exhibition.

In an unprecedented time, when a global pandemic has confined us in our homes for many months, we perhaps understand and treasure these paintings all the more for their introspection and beauty.

Lynn Marsden-Atlass
Executive Director and University Curator

Pieter Cornelisz van Slingelandt, *Portrait of a Man Reading a Book*, 1668, oil on copper, 6 ⅜ × 5 in. (16.2 × 12.6 cm). The Leiden Collection, New York.

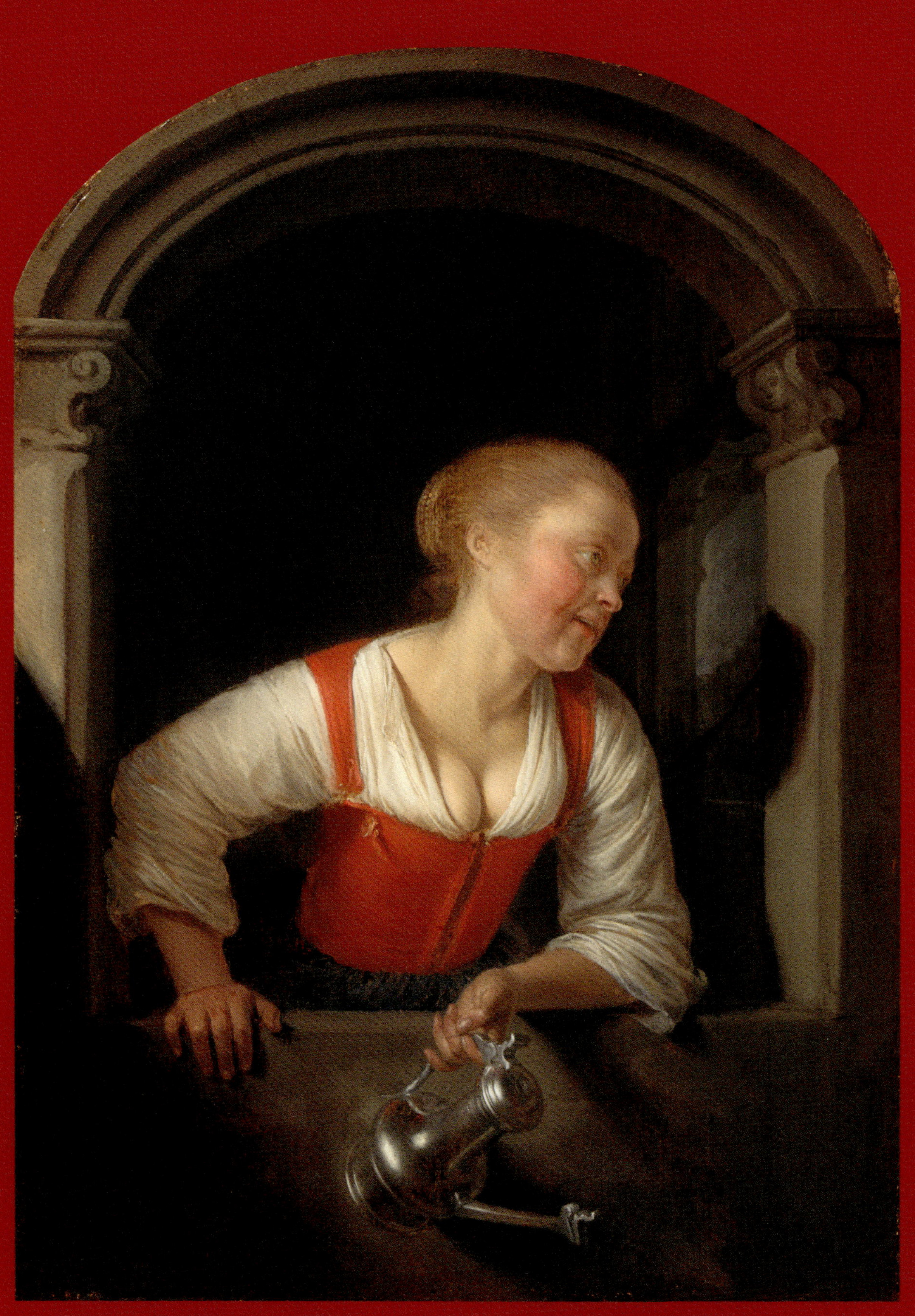

ACKNOWLEDGMENTS

On behalf of the Arthur Ross Gallery, I extend our hearty gratitude to The Leiden Collection, in New York, our partner in organizing this catalogue and its related exhibition. Particular thanks to Thomas S. Kaplan and Daphne Recanati Kaplan for making this remarkable collection available for the public to enjoy through exhibitions such as *An Inner World: Seventeenth-Century Dutch Genre Painting*. We thank Lara Yeager-Crasselt, curator of The Leiden Collection, for agreeing to offer this new iteration of her exhibition of the same title first mounted at the Sterling and Francine Clark Art Institute in Williamstown, Massachusetts, in 2017. Kathleen Morris, director of exhibitions and collections and curator of decorative arts at the Clark, graciously allowed us to use the exhibition's original title and lent Gerrit Dou's *Girl at a Window* (cat. 1) to this reprise of *An Inner World* at the Ross Gallery. The University of Pennsylvania's Kislak Center for Special Collections, Books, and Manuscripts has also been a generous partner, lending nine rare books to this exhibition. Our thanks to John Pollack and Nicholas Herman for providing access to these works, and to Sarah Reidell and the Kislak's conservation lab for ensuring the continued preservation of these important artifacts.

We are grateful to the authors of the three essays published in this volume: Lara Yeager-Crasselt, Shira Brisman, and Eric Jorink. Their original texts, composed for this catalogue, offer new perspectives on the works of the Dutch *fijnschilders* and on seventeenth-century life in Leiden. We also thank Caroline Van Cauwenberge, curatorial associate and digital content coordinator at The Leiden Collection, for translating the Dutch titles of the exhibition's rare books and for authoring biographies of the six painters included in the exhibition. This catalogue was edited by Kristin Swan, and we thank her for crafting a cohesive voice and style for the publication. We offer thanks to Cooper Graphic Design and Brilliant Graphics for this volume's dynamic design and the fine printing that brings this collection of essays and illustrations to life.

Support from the Netherland-America Foundation and the David J. Evans Exhibition Fund made this catalogue possible. Additional support for the exhibition at the Arthur Ross Gallery was provided by the J & AR Foundation, Bill and Kathie Hohns, and the Patron's Circle. In closing, I would like to acknowledge that all of these contributors have offered their voices and expertise under the highly unusual circumstances of quarantine during the COVID-19 pandemic. Thanks to everyone who made space in their own "inner world" to bring this exhibition and catalogue to fruition.

Heather Moqtaderi
Assistant Director and Curator, Arthur Ross Gallery

Gerrit Dou, *Girl at a Window*, ca. 1655, oil on panel, 10 9/16 × 7 ½ in. (26.9 × 19 cm). The Sterling and Francine Clark Art Institute, Williamstown, Massachusetts, 1955.716.

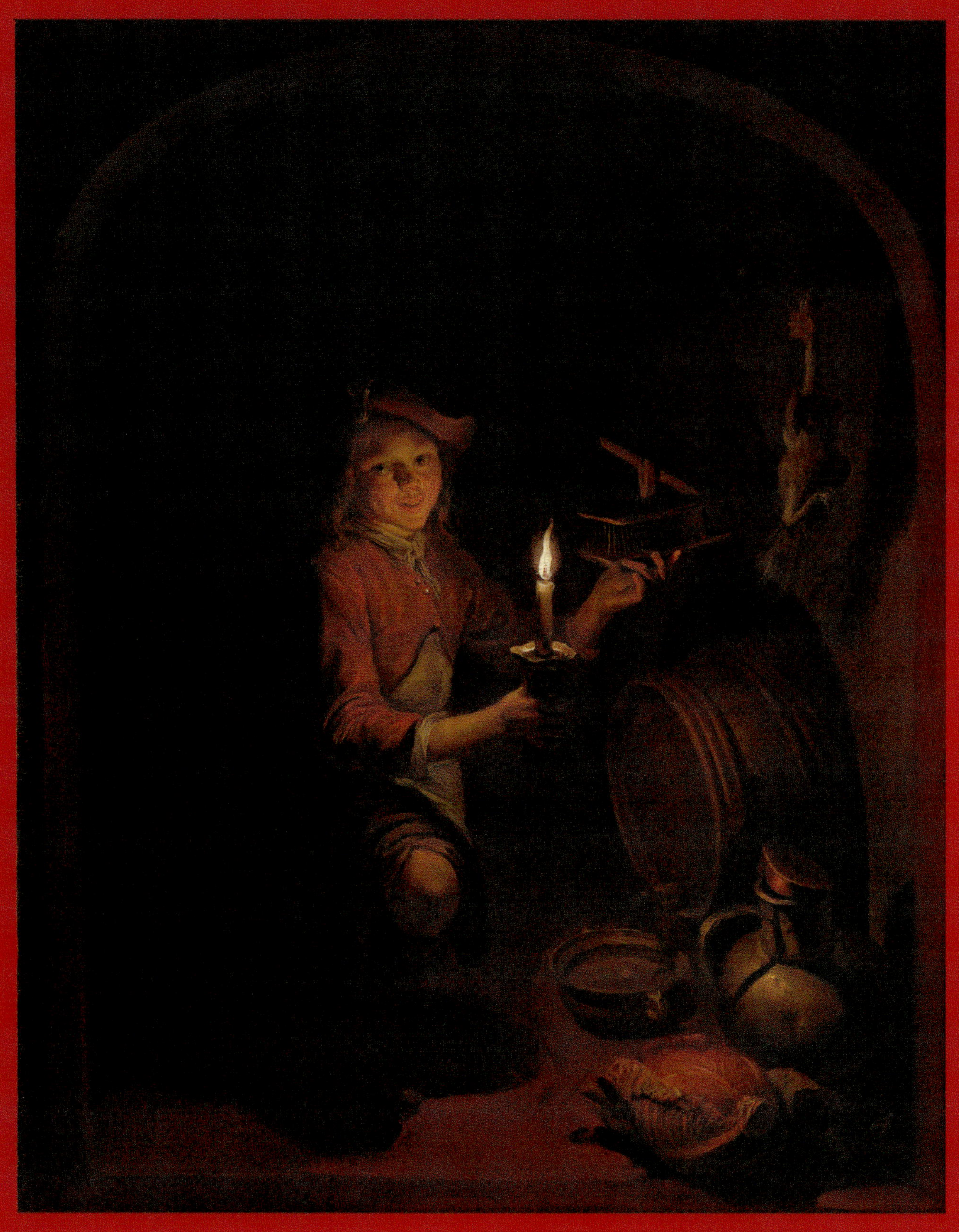

This exhibition originated in an idea to explore the character of intimacy, quiet, and inner reflection as it emerged in a group of seventeenth-century Dutch genre paintings, as well as the ways in which the experience of close looking reinforced these very themes. A special impetus for the first iteration of *An Inner World: Seventeenth-Century Dutch Genre Painting*, at the Sterling and Francine Clark Art Institute in 2017, was Gerrit Dou's painting *Girl at a Window*, which at the time had been recently conserved and reinstalled in the Clark galleries. The exhibition brought Dou's painting into dialogue with a group of exceptional loans from The Leiden Collection that offered an opportunity to examine and query these ideas in various ways. I would like to express my gratitude to Kathleen Morris, as well as my former colleagues at the Clark, for generously supporting this exhibition in each of its iterations.

The expanded and reimagined exhibition at the Arthur Ross Gallery would not have happened without the enthusiasm of Heather Moqtaderi, who wrote me in the summer of 2018 with the idea of presenting this show in Philadelphia. I am grateful to Heather for our warm and productive collaboration over these past few years, as well as for the support of Lynn Marsden-Atlass, the team at the Arthur Ross Gallery, and the Kislak Center for Special Collections, Books, and Manuscripts, whose loans have enriched the show. Shira Brisman has been a valuable contributor to the exhibition and the catalogue, as well as a generous colleague. At The Leiden Collection, Caroline Van Cauwenberge has cheerfully helped along the way, and Sara Smith has smoothly guided the loan process. Finally, I would like to express my gratitude to Thomas S. Kaplan and Daphne Recanati Kaplan for making this all possible with their mission of sharing the collection. When this exhibition took shape, I could not have imagined what our present reality would look like, but I hope that, in this new context, the small, quiet worlds depicted in these Dutch paintings provide places for thought and reflection, respite and inspiration.

Lara Yeager-Crasselt
Curator, The Leiden Collection

Domenicus van Tol, *Boy with a Mousetrap by Candlelight*, ca. 1664–65, oil on panel, 11 ¹³⁄₁₆ × 9 ³⁄₁₆ in. (30 × 23.3 cm). The Leiden Collection, New York.

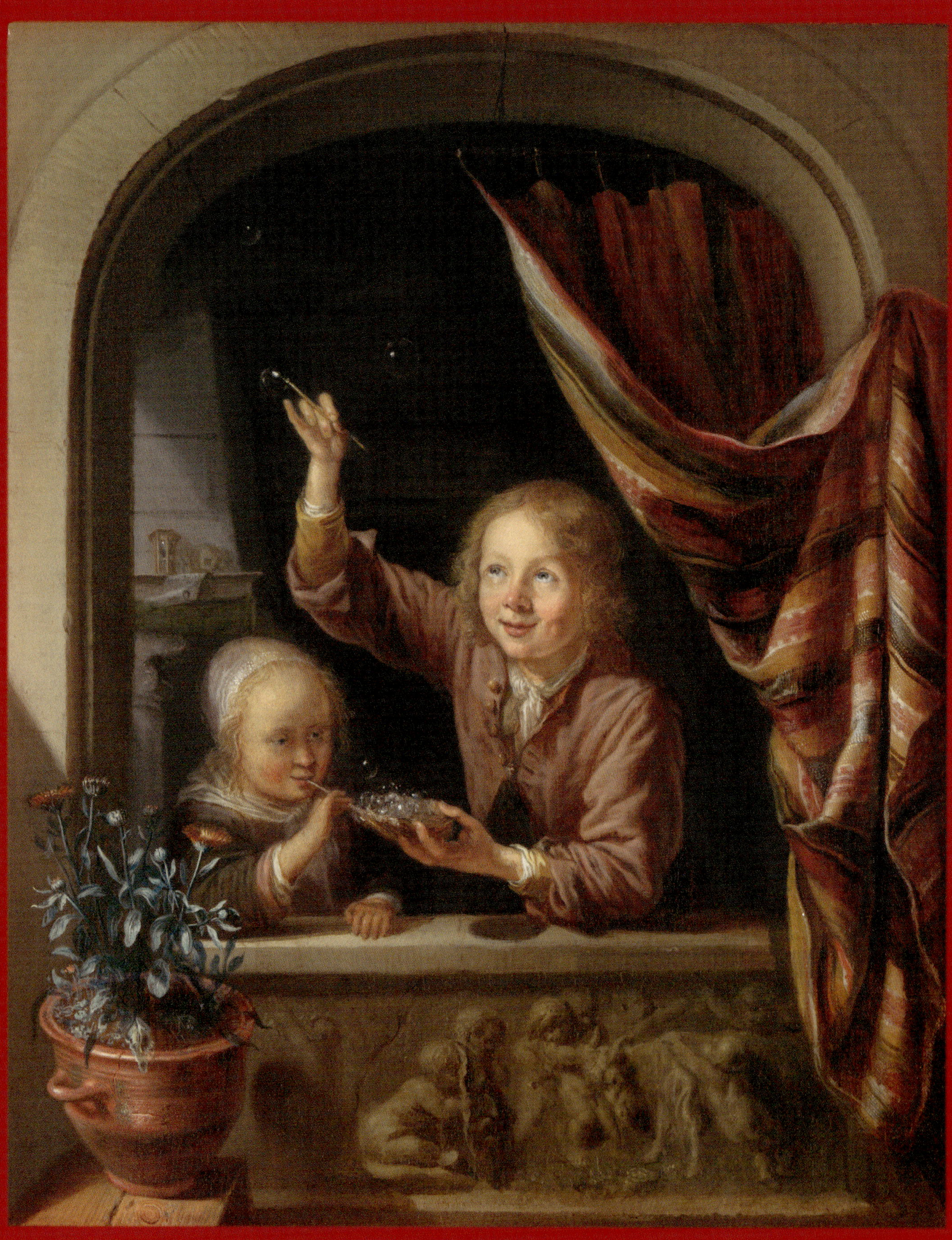

Pulling Back the Curtain

Heather Moqtaderi

The exhibition *An Inner World: Seventeenth-Century Dutch Genre Painting* offers a window into the intellectual and domestic lives of men and women in the Dutch city of Leiden in the 1600s. Alongside a selection of manuscripts from the period, this exhibition brings together a small but diverse group of paintings that investigate the private and public lives of individuals, many posed within window niches. These views offer the finely detailed portrayal of figures and architectural spaces characteristic of Dutch Golden Age painting, often blended with symbolic and historical references to be decoded by the erudite viewer. For example, in Domenicus van Tol's *Children at a Window Blowing Bubbles* (cat. 8), the iridescent spheres are as much a demonstration of the painter's virtuosity as an object of youthful joy. Yet two age-old reminders of mortality visible in the background—a skull and an hour-glass—remind us that such pleasures are fleeting. The household items are symbolic devices rather than a realistic portrayal of domestic decorations, more closely related to the religious philosophy of the mind than the material world of the home's interior.

The three essays in this catalogue deeply consider the concepts of public and private life in seventeenth-century Leiden through the lens of paintings and printed books produced and studied by the city's artists and scholars. By the 1650s, Leiden University had long been established as a major European center for learning. It boasted one of the first anatomical theaters in Europe, drawing crowds to witness public dissections as well as to explore the university's on-site cabinet of curiosities. Students of medicine and science likewise had access to one of the oldest botanical gardens in the world. Along with the university's observatory and famed library, these resources fostered a rich academic and artistic community and shaped civic life during the Age of Enlightenment. The essays in *An Inner World* investigate and interrogate selected works of the Leiden *fijnschilders* (fine painters) within this cultural context, where the pursuit of knowledge through keen observation and reflection was a cherished value.

Lara Yeager-Crasselt begins her essay with Gabriel Metsu's *Woman Reading a Book by a Window* (cat. 4), drawing our attention to the sitter's "antique" robe

Domenicus van Tol, *Children at a Window Blowing Bubbles*, ca. 1660 , oil on panel, 10 ⁷⁄₁₆ × 8 ¹⁄₁₆ in. (26.5 × 20.5 cm). The Leiden Collection, New York.

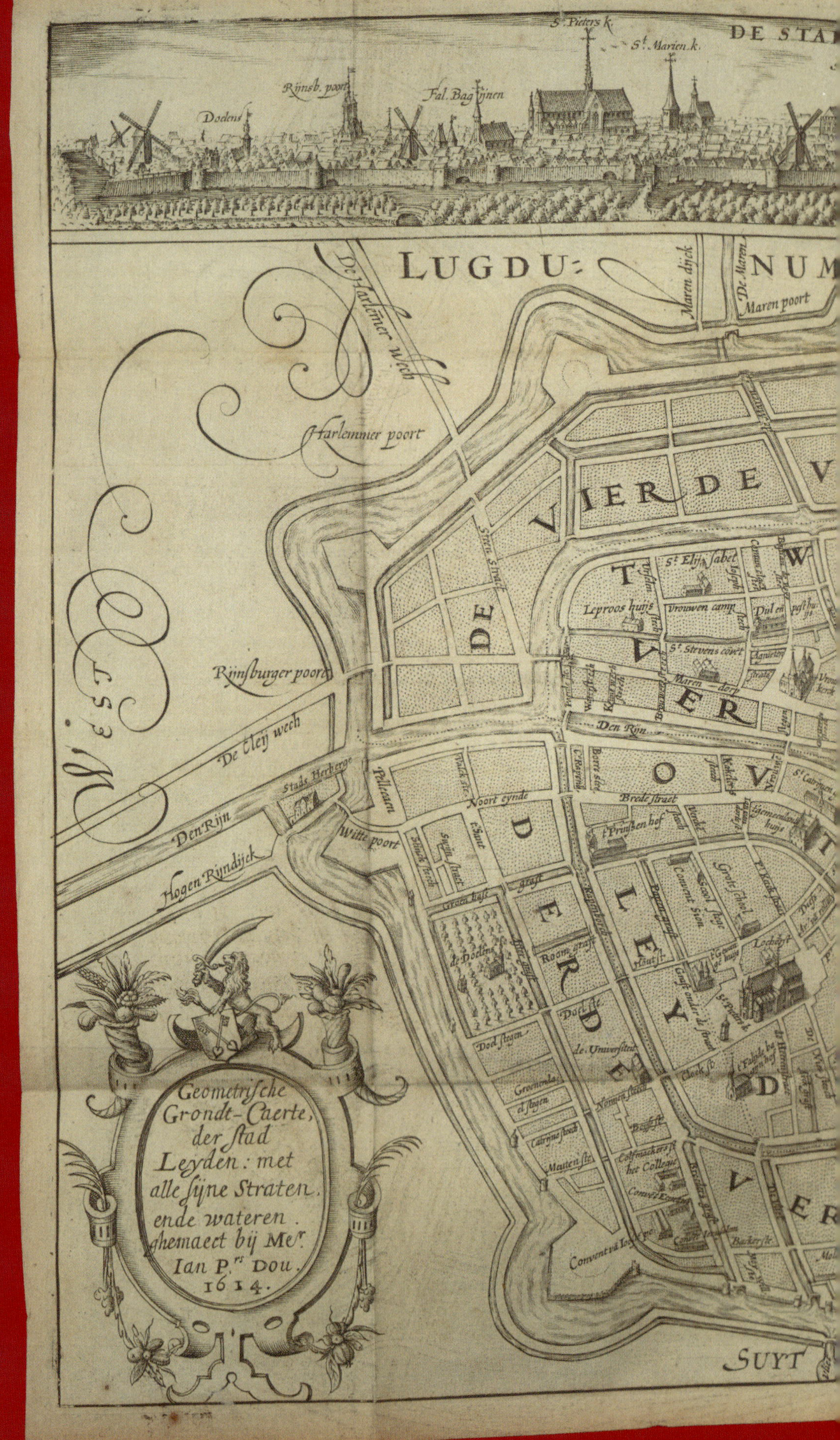

DE STA
S. Pieters k.
S. Marien k.
Rijnsb. poort
Val. Bagijnen
Doelen
LUGDU:
NUM
Maren dijck
De Maren
Maren poort
De Harlemer Wech
Harlemmer poort
VIERDE V
DE
T
S. Elisabet
W
Leproos huijs
Vrouwen camp
Dul en pest hu
S. Steuens coort
Amsterd.
strate
V
Maren dam
VER
Den Rijn
OV
Rijnsburger poort
Breestraet
S. Catrin
De Cley wech
Noort eynde
Brede straet
t Prinssen hof
Pellican
Stads Herberge
Groote schol
Convent Sun
Den Rijn
Hogen Rijndijck
Witte poort
DE
LEY
Roome
De Doelen
DER
Dodt stegh
de Universiteyt
LEY
Groenwate
el stegen
Caron me fteeg
Bassteyt
Matten str.
Caffmackers
het Collegi
Convent
VER
Geometrische
Grondt-Caerte,
der stad
Leyden: met
alle sijne Straten.
ende wateren
ghemaect bij Mer.
Ian P.rs Dou.
1614.
WEST
SUYT

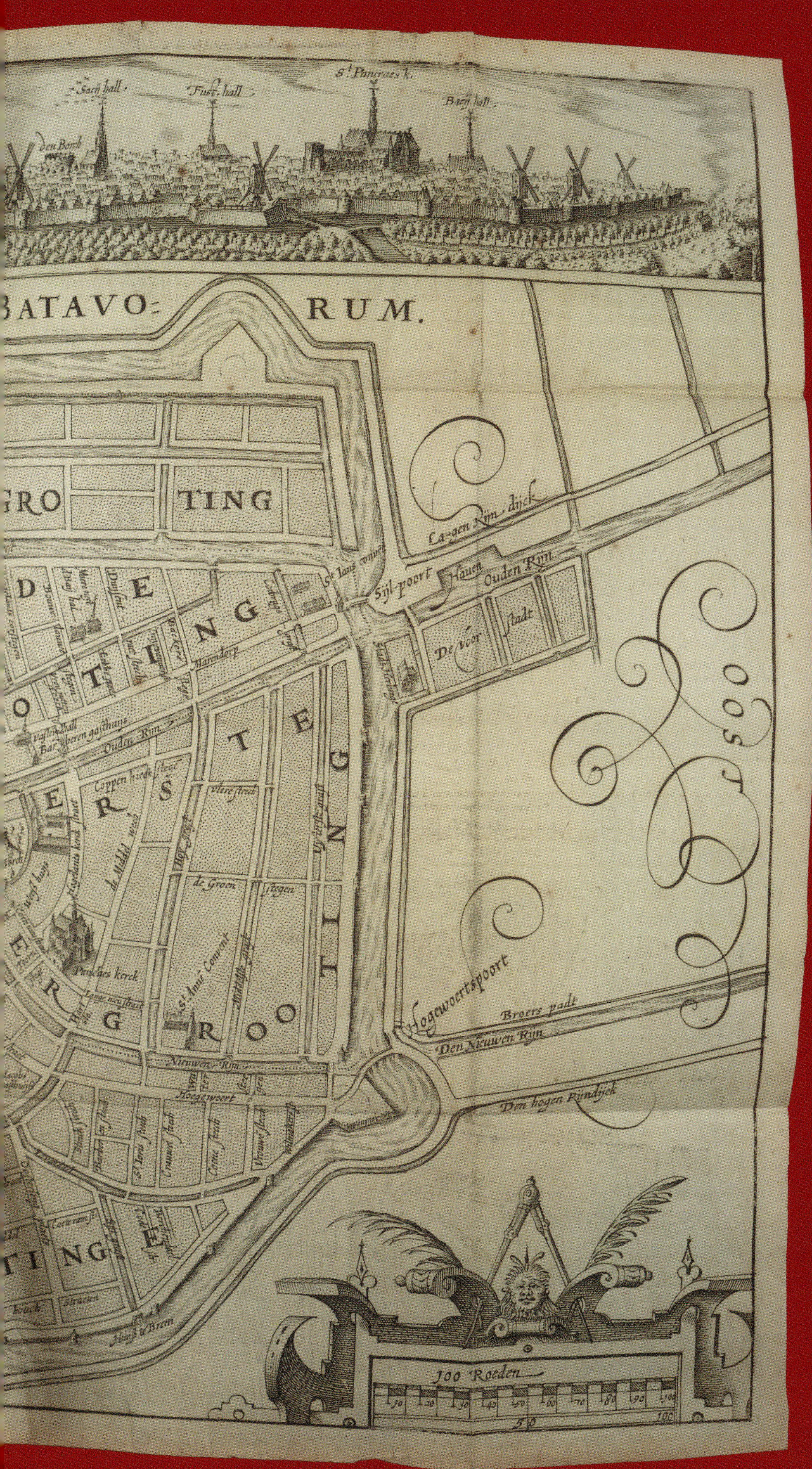

Sacr. hall.
Fust. hall.
S.t Pancraes k.
Baer. hall.
den Borch
BATAVO—RUM.
GRO TING
DE TING
ROOTING
ERSTE
RG ROOTING
TING E
La-gen Rijn-dijck
de lang convet
Sijl-poort
Hauen
Ouden Rijn
De Voor stadt
Stadts Herbarg
Marendorp
Duyssē
Vishal
Barberen gasthuijs
Ouden-Rijn
Coppen hiecks stegt
vlere strech
de Groen stegen
Pancras kerck
Hogewoertspoort
Broers padt
Den Nieuwen Rijn
Nieuwen-Rijn
Hoogewoert
Den hogen Rijndijck
Straten
Huijs te Brem
100 Roeden
10 20 30 40 50 60 70 80 90 100
50
100

along with the books and letters surrounding her, which reference scholarly endeavors. In this exceptional painting, Metsu departs from the smaller scale and finely detailed brushwork of Leiden's *fijnschilders*, using a looser, more expressive technique to portray his subject. Yeager-Crasselt proceeds to describe how the characteristics of the city of Leiden fostered thematic richness and diversity in the works of Metsu and his contemporaries. Her essay traces the relationship between the university city's professors, publishers, and artists to illustrate how Leiden's cultural climate contributed to high levels of scholarly and artistic achievement. By closely examining period works such as Gerrit Dou's *Scholar Interrupted at His Writing* (see fig. 2.4), Yeager-Crasselt illustrates the ways in which artists present public and private space in portrayals of "learned" professions. Using the exceptional example of Metsu's "learned lady," Yeager-Crasselt also considers the changing attitudes toward female intellectuals in seventeenth-century Leiden.

Shira Brisman builds on Yeager-Crasselt's interpretation of Metsu's painting, comparing *Woman Reading a Book by a Window* and the artist's *Public Notary* (cat. 3) through the lens of letter writing and record keeping, respectively. The subject of Metsu's *Woman Reading* is seen from within a domestic interior, her unsealed correspondence tucked in the windowpane behind her. She achieves intellectual and emotional satisfaction through the act of sending and receiving letters, which serve as intermediaries between the subject's isolated interior world and the public realm. Brisman argues that the pictorial convention of depicting women reading letters, often seated before a window, reveals the covert, inward-looking nature of women's intellectual life at this time. In contrast, Brisman presents Metsu's notary as a civic figure and "namer of things" in his role in classifying information. Viewed from the street,

he leans out an open window to present the viewer with his ledger. Brisman compares windows to wax seals as mediators of private and public space. She situates both of these subjects within Leiden's mercantile economy, drawing our attention to the ways that indviduals asserted power through letter writing and record keeping within private and public spheres.

Eric Jorink connects the *fijnschilders'* interest in detail with the emerging practice of scientific inquiry in the seventeenth century. Linking fine painting with science, he presents the two disciplines' affinities with Leiden's famous textile industry, noting a shared preoccupation with texture, structure, and sensory perception in all three fields. Jorink describes the invention of the microscope as promoting increased attention to minute structures, as exemplified by medical professor and art collector Franciscus de la Boë Sylvius, who studied the barely visible inner structure of the human body. His scientific work included alchemical research, which was at the time a respected field of inquiry as well as a pathway to divine knowledge. But as Jorink details, Sylvius's interests extended beyond the scientific realm. An inventory of Sylvius's house documented a vast collection that included paintings by the *fijnschilders* along with other works of art, exotic objects, valuable textiles, chemical utensils, and an array of scientific instruments.

These three essays offer fresh perspectives on intellectual life in Leiden during the Dutch Golden Age. The authors pull back the curtain on works by the *fijnschilders*, allowing us to closely examine the painters' representation of public and private life. As noted throughout this volume, the seventeenth-century Dutch academic capital experienced the simultaneous flourishing of printed books, letter writing, and scientific discovery. In his 1614 map

Jan Pietersz, *De Stad Leyden (The City of Leiden)*, 1614, engraving, 11 ¹¹⁄₁₆ × 14 ⅝ in. (29.6 × 37.1 cm). Pasted in Johannes van Meurs, *Illustris Academia Lugd-Batava (The Illustrious Academy of Lugd-Batavia)* (Leiden: Andream Cloucquium, 1613). Kislak Center for Special Collections, Rare Books, and Manuscripts, University of Pennsylvania, Philadelphia.

The City of Leiden, Jan Pietersz depicts the Netherlands' second-largest city as a center for Protestant religious study and university learning. We can locate Leiden University's buildings and grounds in the southwest corner, just west of Pieterskerk and the Rapenburg canal. Pasted neatly into Johannes van Meurs's *Illustris Academia Lugd-Batava* (cat. 14), Pietersz's map unfolds as an inner world, inviting us to consider the lives of those who walked these streets and inhabited these spaces.

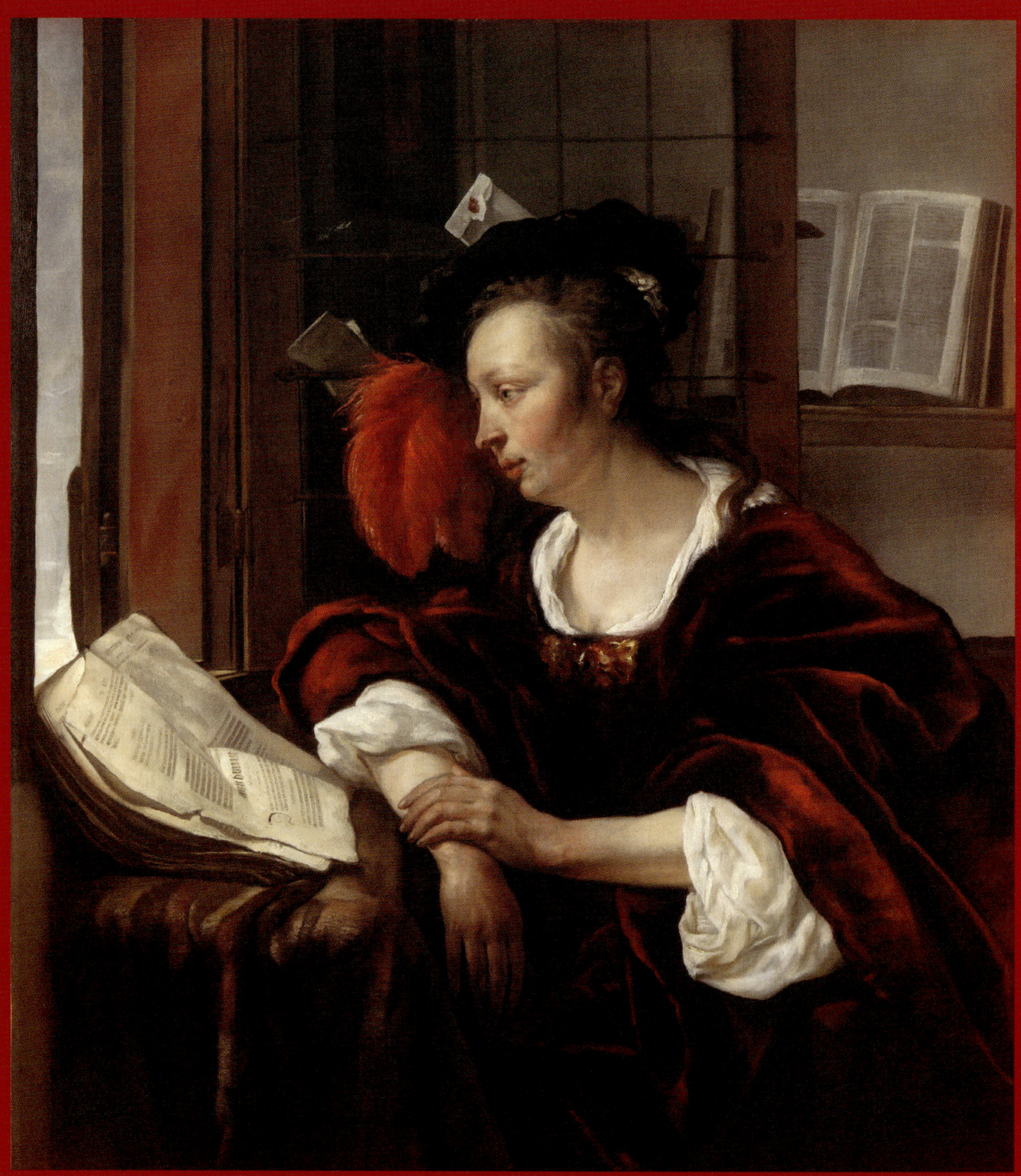

Embracing an Inner World in Seventeenth-Century Dutch Genre Painting

Lara Yeager-Crasselt

Gabriel Metsu (1629–1667) executed his ambitious *Woman Reading a Book by a Window* (cat. 4) in his native Leiden in the early 1650s, shortly before leaving this prosperous university town for Amsterdam, its larger neighbor to the north.[1] The subject would have resonated within Leiden's scholarly milieu. The young woman, dressed in a voluminous red velvet robe, white blouse, and scarlet-plumed black beret—a form of historicizing or "antique" costume—raises her eyes from the text that she has been reading.[2] With one elbow she leans forward, resting her arm as a bright, warm light illuminates the room and emphasizes her wide eyes and distinctive features. The large book is propped against the windowsill; its well-worn pages— even slightly torn on the left side—indicate frequent use. A second book opened on the ledge behind the sitter and two letters tucked under the window's mullions emphasize the seriousness of her scholarly endeavors. In this dedicated space for study and thought, the physical stillness of the moment is met by the fullness of an inner life.

Metsu's depiction of this female scholar was exceptional in the mid-seventeenth century, when women were rarely, if ever, portrayed engaged in intellectual study.[3] Yet, even though she sits in a domestic interior that seems to be drawn from daily life, her distinctive dress removes her from a specific time and place.[4] This tension underscores the compelling character of Metsu's image: it is at once immediate and abstract, negotiating broader concepts of learning and knowledge embodied in the figure of the scholar herself.

While this painting is distinguished among contemporaneous works in Leiden for its subject matter, painterly brushwork, and monumentality— it measures nearly three by three feet—Metsu was by no means alone in his ability to depict a scene defined by an intimacy of thought and action.[5] A number of artists in Leiden who are featured in this exhibition, including Gerrit Dou (1613–1675), Domenicus van Tol (ca. 1635–1676), Pieter Cornelisz van Slingelandt (1640–1691), Jacob Toorenvliet (1640–1719), and Willem van Mieris (1662–1747), showed a similar interest in the depiction of figures in interior spaces engaged in study, contemplation, or quiet exchange.[6] Their works show an awareness of the artistic potential of a pictorial world focused inward, where the positive associations of Leiden's intellectual culture could take shape in expansive and integrated ways. At the same

Gabriel Metsu, *Woman Reading a Book by a Window*, ca. 1653–54, oil on canvas, 41 5/16 × 35 3/4 in. (105 × 90.7 cm). The Leiden Collection, New York.

time, the small scale and refined nature of this group of "fine paintings," with their attention to detail, effects of light and shadow, and use of fictive window ledges or frames, achieve a pictorial illusionism that enhances the beholder's engagement with the painting as a physical object.[7]

Leiden offered a distinctive cultural and artistic environment for the development of these ideas in the seventeenth century. Home to the United Provinces' first university, which had been founded in 1575 by William of Orange, Leiden identified with its intellectual traditions and academic community. By the 1640s, the city also became known as a center of *fijnschilders* (fine painters) as a result of Gerrit Dou's thematic and stylistic innovations in genre painting. His manner of painting "small, subtle, and curious things," as the Leiden historian Jan Jansz Orlers (1570–1646) remarked in 1641,[8] made Dou one of the most admired and successful artists in the Dutch Republic. Dou trained a number of pupils over the course of his career—Toorenvliet, Van Tol, and Van Slingelandt among them—impacting a generation of artists who sustained the taste for fine painting into the eighteenth century.[9]

By exploring the major themes of this exhibition through the lens of Leiden's intellectual and artistic traditions, this essay investigates how the city's local character contributed to and sustained artists' innovative and varied expressions of an inner world. It suggests that this framework not only impacted artists' choice of subject matter, but also, more broadly, fostered an interest in capturing its thematic richness and diversity. While this discussion focuses on the group of paintings and rare books included in *An Inner World*, it also addresses some of the larger concerns raised by this subject matter, such as the evocation of time and temporality, the role of pictorial illusionism in activating the experience of the beholder, and the gendered spaces of learning and knowledge.

ENDEAVORS OF THE MIND AND THE HAND: LEIDEN'S SCHOLARLY AND ARTISTIC TRADITIONS

By the mid-seventeenth century, Leiden University had long been a thriving intellectual hub. Its founding in the wake of the Netherlands revolt—and thus as the first university of the newly independent, and Calvinist, northern provinces—tied it strongly to the city's identity.[10] The university quickly rose to become one of the most important centers of learning in Protestant Europe and attracted leading thinkers early on, such as the Flemish philologist Justus Lipsius, the French historian Joseph Justus Scaliger, the French theologian Franciscus Junius the Elder, and the French botanist Carolus Clusius. Students, too, came from near and far to undertake studies in philosophy, rhetoric, theology, and linguistics, as well as to attend the famed Theatrum Anatomicum (anatomical theater) or visit the Hortus Botanicus (botanical garden).[11] In 1658, the university faculty welcomed the renowned professor of medicine Franciscus de la Boë Sylvius, a figure known for his clinical teachings, anatomical dissections, and chemical theories, as well as for his patronage of the Leiden *fijnschilders*.[12]

As the university continued to expand, so did Leiden's publishing industry and flourishing book culture, evident in the university's own important library (FIG. 2.1).[13] Spurred by the great influx of Flemish immigrants who arrived as religious exiles in the late sixteenth century, Leiden's publishing community grew rapidly. Beginning with the establishment of the Leidse Officina Plantiniana by the Antwerp printer Christoffel Plantin (ca. 1520–1589) in 1563, the city would come to have several hundred printers over the course of the

FIG. 2.1. Willem Isaacsz van Swanenburg, after Jan Cornelisz van 't Woudt, *Library of Leiden University*, 1610, etching and engraving, 13 × 15 ⅞ in. (33 × 40.3 cm). Rijksmuseum, Amsterdam, RP-P-1893-A-18092.

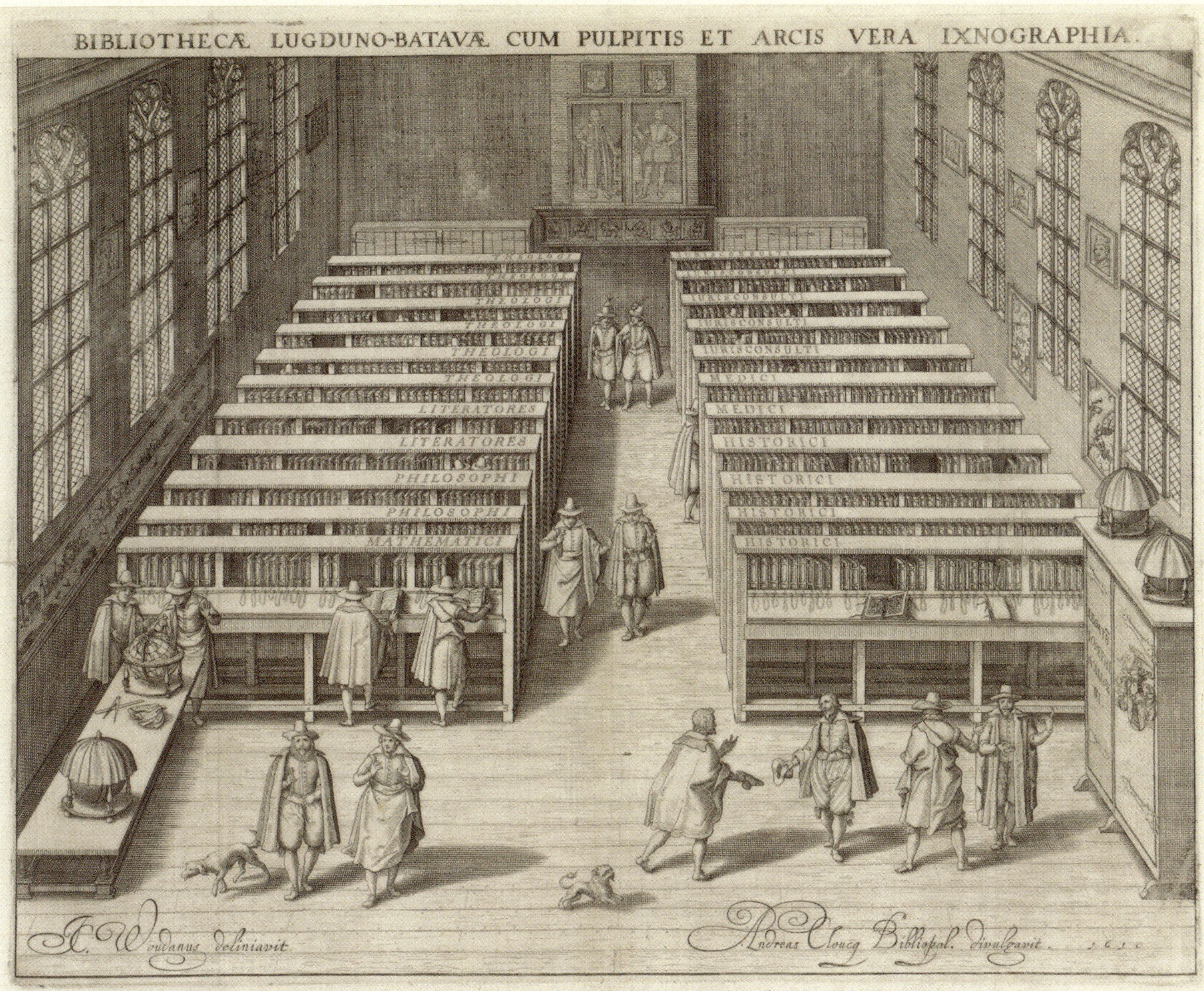

BIBLIOTHECÆ LUGDUNO-BATAVÆ CUM PULPITIS ET ARCIS VERA IXNOGRAPHIA.
THEOLOGI
THEOLOGI
THEOLOGI
THEOLOGI
LITERATORES
LITERATORES
PHILOSOPHI
PHILOSOPHI
MATHEMATICI
IURISCONSULTI
IURISCONSULTI
IURISCONSULTI
MEDICI
MEDICI
HISTORICI
HISTORICI
HISTORICI
HISTORICI
J. Woudanus deliniavit
Andreas Cloucq Bibliopol. divulgavit. 1610

PHLIPS ANGELS
LOF
DER
SCHILDER-KONST.

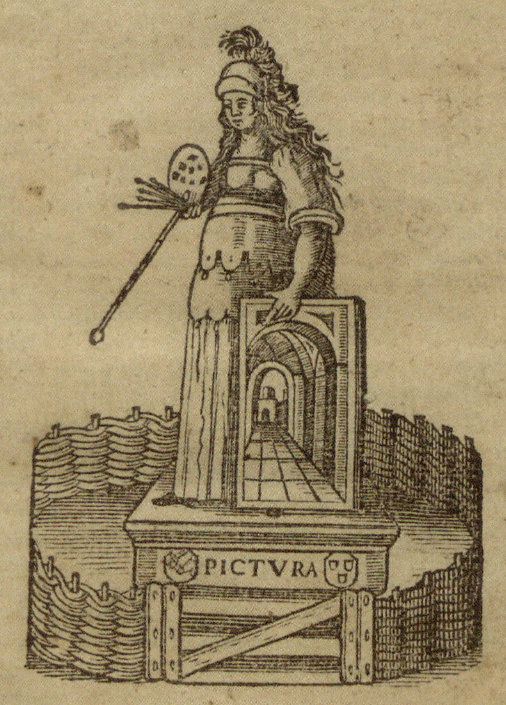

TOT LEYDEN,

Ghedruckt by *Willem Christiaens*, woonende by de Academie. ANNO 1642.

seventeenth and eighteenth centuries.[14] While literacy rates were high throughout the Netherlands—by 1650 about half of the adult population could read and write—it is difficult to determine more precisely what books people owned.[15] Religious and devotional texts were popular—above all the Bible, which was translated into Dutch in 1618 (cat. 15), and its illustrated counterpart, the *Bible moraliseé* (cat. 13)—along with classical texts and emblem books, especially those by the writer and moralist Jacob Cats (cat. 12).[16] The ubiquity of books in Leiden's culture helps to explain their frequent appearance in the work of Leiden artists, including many throughout this exhibition. As a visual motif, moreover, the book's significance was multifold: while it represented the city's culture of learning and knowledge, it also served as a reminder that the book functioned as a physical object that was meant to be held, used, and displayed.[17]

One of the most significant books published in Leiden in this period was Jan Jansz Orlers's *Beschrijvinge der stad Leyden* (*Description of the City of Leiden*), which appeared in two editions in 1614 and 1641. Orlers's text chronicled Leiden's past and present, including the lives of its "illustrious, learned and renowned men."[18] In his second edition, Orlers included biographies of Leiden's scholars, long a source of its pride, alongside a number of artists, including contemporaries like Dou.[19] As Orlers himself explained, Leiden had "not been idle in nurturing and rearing in equal measure [in comparison to scholars] many and various artists: especially . . . many renowned and excellent painters."[20] They had become a key aspect of the city's profile and formed part of its distinctive local identity.[21]

The ties between Leiden's scholars and artists— a rhetorical strategy that bolstered the reputation of both—emerged in the work of another native painter and printmaker in 1642. Philips Angel's *Lof der Schilderkonst* (*Praise in the Art of Painting*), which followed a speech Angel gave to the city's painters in 1641, sought to defend the dignity of the painter's profession.[22] Like Orlers, Angel acknowledged Leiden's dual strengths, expressing how "our art . . . makes Leiden, which is a breeding ground for all great minds, even more illustrious."[23] The title page of the treatise (FIG. 2.2) is an apt representation of these intersecting traditions. Angel adapted and merged two existing vignettes—one from a Leiden printer and the other from the title page of Samuel Marolois's treatise on perspective (Amsterdam, 1638)—with the symbol of the university: the goddess Minerva.[24] The resulting print depicts a female figure standing in an enclosed garden, a palette, brushes, and maulstick having replaced the book, shield, and sword ordinarily associated with the goddess. Here, she is the embodiment of *pictura*, taking her place as an emblem of Leiden's glory.[25]

EMBODYING AN INNER WORLD: SAINTS, SCHOLARS, ART LOVERS, AND ALCHEMISTS

Even earlier, however, artists had begun to respond to the city's scholarly milieu in various ways. One of the first indications of this impact appears in a group of paintings depicting biblical apostles and evangelists by Jan Lievens (1607–1674) and Rembrandt van Rijn (1606–1669) in the mid to late 1620s. In Lievens's *Saint Paul* from ca. 1624–25 (FIG. 2.3), for example, the artist rendered the aged, bearded saint in the act of writing, gazing down at the pages of the folio before him with pen raised in mid-thought. Rembrandt altered the narrative and thematic moment in *Saint Paul in Prison* (1627, Staatsgalerie Stuttgart), where the saint, though surrounded by stacks of thick volumes, is entirely absorbed in his own spiritual contemplations.[26] Lievens's and Rembrandt's portrayals of Saint Paul as

a

FIG. 2.2. Anonymous, title page of Philips Angel, *Lof der Schilderkonst* (*Praise in the Art of Painting*), Leiden, 1642. Leiden University Library, Leiden, 21220 F 38.

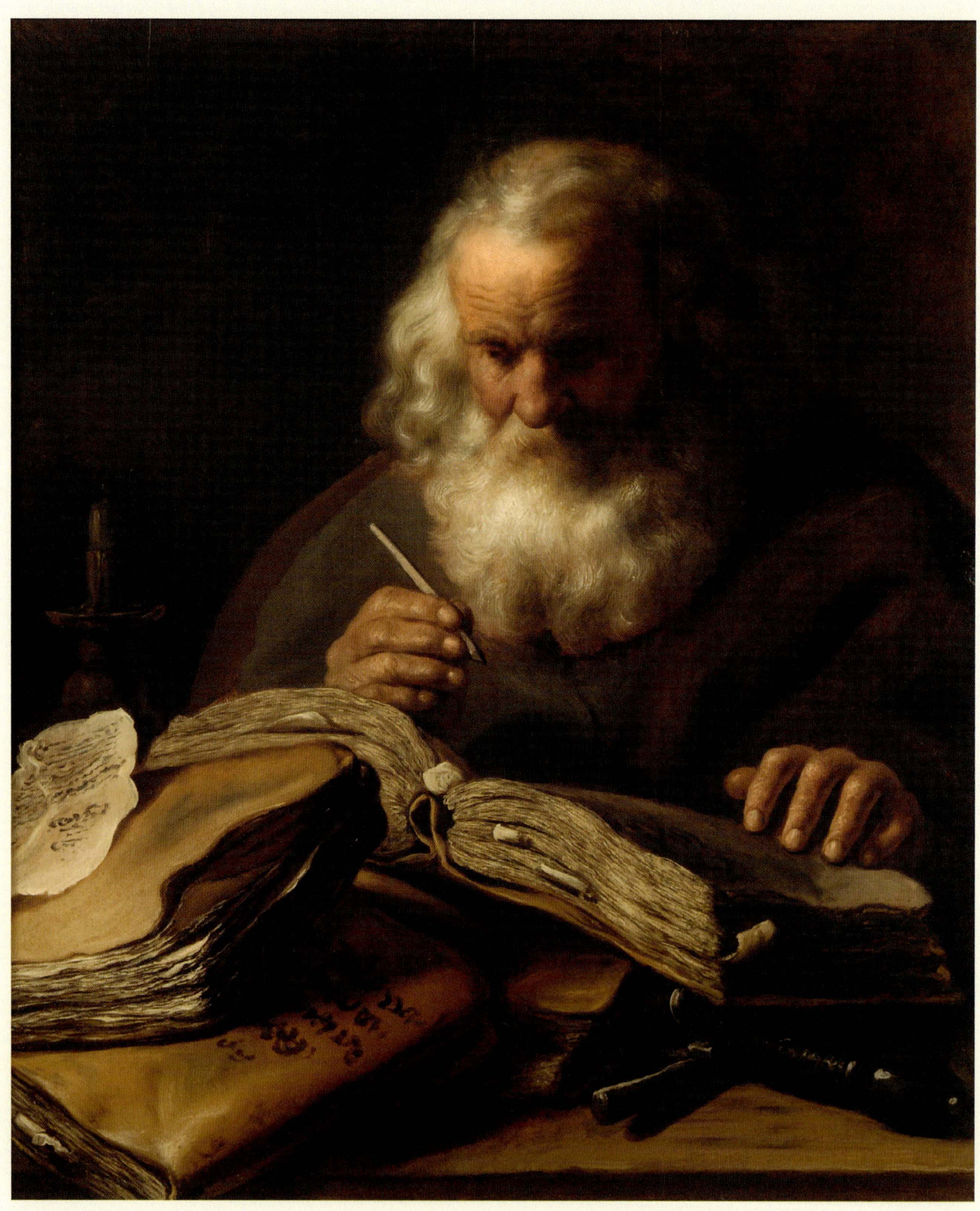

religious scholar—a subject they depicted on numerous occasions—reflected the importance that Protestants placed on a direct engagement with the written word, as well as an interest in capturing the intellectual labor and humility that accompanied their divine revelations.[27] This approach would have likely appealed to Leiden's Protestant intellectual community, especially one that was at the center of the divisive religious debates that took place within the Dutch Reformed Church in the first quarter of the century.[28] In this climate, Lievens's and Rembrandt's paintings carried a heightened historical immediacy.

Gerrit Dou, who first came to study with Rembrandt in 1628, explored scholarly themes throughout his career, demonstrating the virtues of intellectual endeavor.[29] In one of his early paintings of this subject matter from ca. 1635, *Scholar Interrupted at His Writing* (FIG. 2.4), an elderly scholar, wearing a fur-trimmed *tabbaard* and black skullcap, has paused from writing and gazes directly at the viewer.[30] His pen pressed to the page and furrowed brow indicate that his mind is still at work. Although Dou's painting was not intended as a specific portrait, his characterization of the scholar suggests that he was familiar with the collections of engraved portrait prints of renowned Leiden professors that were published in the first quarter of the century.[31] These popular books, such as the *Illustris Academia* (cat. 14), celebrated members of the university's faculty and were sold as souvenirs for visitors to the city.[32]

Dou's meticulously rendered composition—down to the artist's signature that appears tucked into a page in the book—expands and idealizes the motif found in the portrait prints. He not only depicted the scholar at work but, by suspending the figure's thought and movement, also created a temporal narrative moment—that achieves both intimacy and immediacy for the

viewer.[33] We recognize the scholar's arrested action as a form of contemplation and perceive our presence as an interruption of his solitude.[34] The painting's thematic and stylistic innovations modernized one of Leiden's important cultural traditions, showing the rich possibilities of portraying the inner worlds of mind and body.

Dou's contemporaries took up these themes in various ways. Pieter Cornelisz van Slingelandt, whom the Leiden chronicler Simon van Leeuwen described (along with Dou's celebrated pupil Frans van Mieris the Elder) as "equal to their master, and may possibly go on to surpass him," adapted the motif of a man paused from reading in a refined portrait of 1668 (cat. 7).[35] With his right fingers placed between the pages, the sitter gazes expectantly toward the viewer. He wears a skullcap and a fashionable *Japonse rock* (Japanese robe), a garment that had come to be associated with learning.[36] Slingelandt showcases the man's wealth and erudition, presenting him as a modern gentleman-scholar. Jacob Toorenvliet's alchemists (cat. 10), on the other hand, are engaged in a quiet exchange with each other. Alchemy, a kind of pseudo-science and precursor to modern chemistry, involved (among other things) the attempted transmutation of base metals into gold (cat. 19). Toorenvliet's unusually dignified pair—the master alchemist wears a splendid fur-trimmed purple robe resembling a *tabbaard*—discuss the results of an experiment in secret.[37] The various objects in the foreground, including the crumpled pages of well-used books, demonstrate alchemists' reliance on intellectual and practical knowledge. Their work benefitted from the intimacy of their private space, where ideas could be discussed freely and allowed to flourish.[38]

A different dynamic plays out in Metsu's *Public Notary* (cat. 3). Identified by the sign below him—*openbaer*

FIG. 2.3. Jan Lievens, *St. Paul*, ca. 1624–25, oil on panel, 37 × 31 in. (94 × 78.7 cm). Agnes Etherington Art Centre, Queen's University, Kingston, Ontario, Gift of Alfred and Isabel Bader, 2006 (49-002).

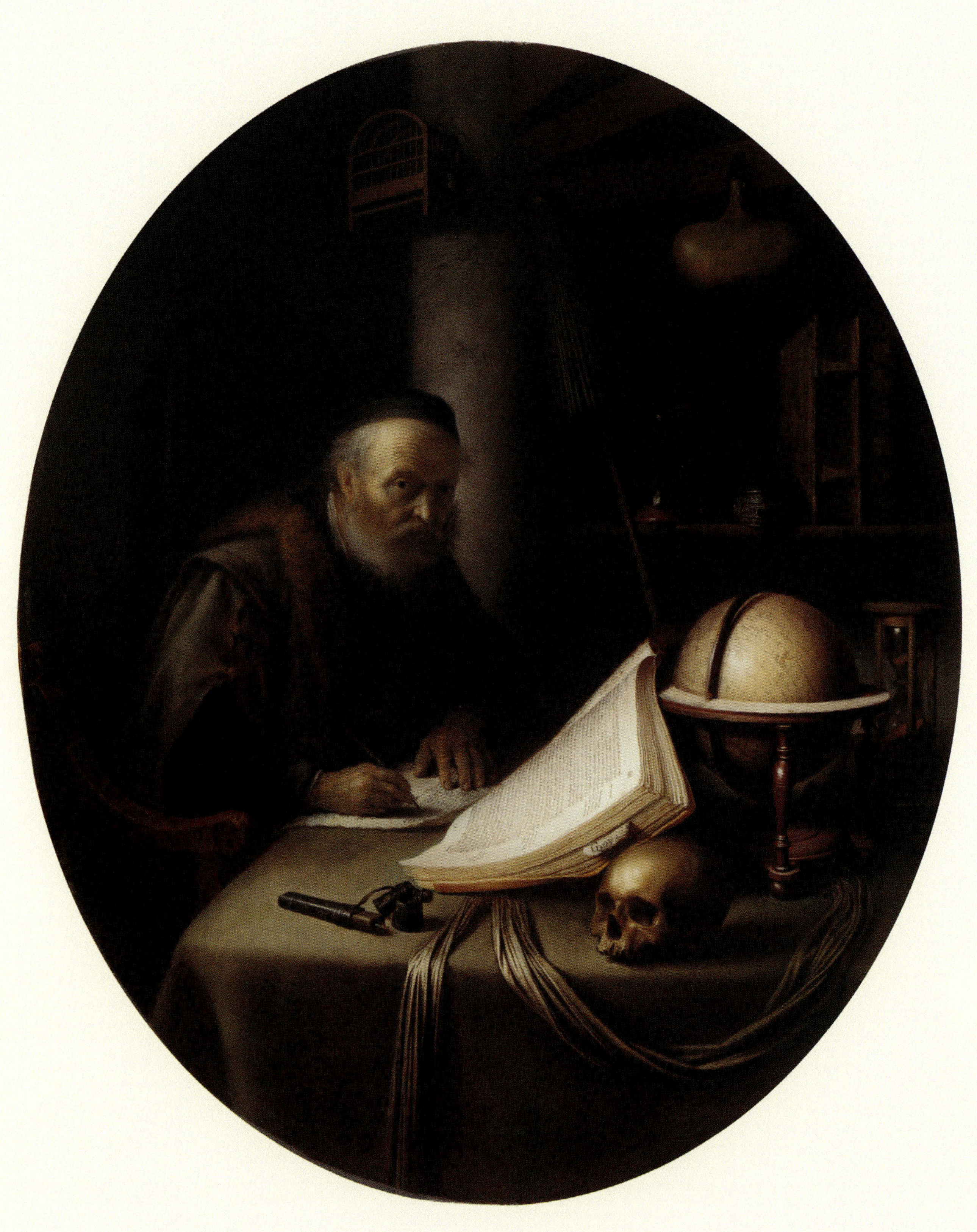

Notarus—Metsu's figure leans out of a stone window ledge and extends his papers, folded and marked with two prominent seals, toward the viewer. With his graying beard and steady expression, the notary evokes the figure of the scholar, instilling a sense of dignity and gravitas into an iconographic tradition often defined by its comic character.[39] This work also represents Metsu's first direct response to Dou's so-called niche pictures (see cats. 1 and 2), in which a figure leans out of a window ledge, seemingly breaking the threshold between real and pictorial space.[40] This motif showcased the artist's technical virtuosity and prompted contemplation on the part of the viewer. As in Metsu's painting, the fictive frame invites a dialogue between "inner" and "outer" worlds, where stilled action and quiet thought meet.

In many ways, Metsu's *Woman Reading a Book by a Window* fits comfortably within Leiden's larger artistic and cultural framework, reflecting the strong intellectual and iconographic traditions that informed the landscape of the city. Here, the reader remains undisturbed by the viewer's presence, and the virtues of the mind and the possibilities of the imagination are on display. Her deep absorption in her thoughts evokes an engraving published by Hendrick Rochusz van Dagen in 1660 (FIG. 2.5), in which a (male) scholar enjoys the pleasures afforded by the solitude of his study.[42] In the accompanying poem, he describes how he finds himself surrounded by "prophets, philosophers, and poets, Greeks and Hebrews; they are capable of teaching him, but are quiet if he asks."[43] This sentiment was already widely known in the Renaissance, evident in the words of the Italian prince and poet Niccolò Machiavelli (1429–1527), who had remarked over a century earlier how "he enjoys nothing more than 'speaking' with the authors of his books in solitude, forgetting the outside world for a few hours."[44]

Metsu's figure has left the outside world behind and entered a space for quiet reflection and thought, yet she is different than her male contemporaries.[45] Seventeenth-century viewers would have recognized that her clothing was distinctly outmoded, and that Metsu likely intended her to represent an allegorical figure personifying understanding or knowledge.[46] The artist would have turned to Cesare Ripa's *Iconologia* (cats. 16 and 17), an influential Italian handbook first published in 1593, which artists often used as a source for allegorical imagery. In the 1644 Dutch edition of Ripa, *Cognitione* (Knowledge) is represented by a woman seated before a large book and holding a torch in her hand.[47] The light illuminates not only her text but also the ideas taking shape in her mind. The natural light that enters the window in Metsu's painting may serve a similar purpose, becoming, as Adriaan E. Waiboer has remarked, "the source of her physical and spiritual illumination."[48]

Still, we must ask why Metsu would have created an allegorical painting of a female scholar in this large-scale format. In the early 1650s, before he left Leiden permanently for Amsterdam, Metsu undertook a brief stay in Utrecht, where he studied with the artist Nicolaus Knüpfer (ca. 1603–1655).[49] Knüpfer, as well as other Utrecht artists such as Jan Baptist Weenix (1621–1659), offered Metsu a different artistic model than he would have experienced in Leiden in terms of both style and scale. In Utrecht, Metsu may also have met, or at least been familiar with, Anna Maria van Schurman (1607–1678), the first Dutch woman to attend university, who lived and worked in the city.[50] Her dissertation, "on the Suitability of a Woman's Mind for Scholarship and Letters" (cat. 18), published in Latin in 1641 and followed by its English translation in 1655, addressed the very question of whether or not women should be educated.[51] Van Schurman, also known as the Utrecht "Minerva," corresponded with a

FIG. 2.4. Gerrit Dou, *Scholar Interrupted at His Writing*, ca. 1635, oil on oval panel, 9 ⅝ × 7 ⅞ in. (24.5 × 20 cm). The Leiden Collection, New York.

number of professors at Leiden University, as well as with a network of women within and beyond the Netherlands, including Princess Elisabeth of the Palatinate.[52] Van Schurman was versed in twelve languages and familiar with the subjects taught at Leiden University, such as philosophy, botany, and medicine, as well as the skills of calligraphy and engraving.[53] Although she represents an exceptional instance of a "learned lady" in the seventeenth century, Van Schurman points to a changing attitude toward female learning and the positive associations it could carry.

With its confident handling and imposing physical presence, Metsu's painting serves as a testament to his artistic ambitions and innovation early in his career. Yet it also affirms and celebrates the acquisition of knowledge as embodied through a female figure. The painting's size suggests that Metsu did not make it without a patron in mind, and he may have been commissioned to execute this work by someone associated with the university in Leiden— or perhaps even Utrecht.[54] Like the depictions of an inner world presented in the works in this exhibition, where small interiors, intimate exchanges of knowledge, and suggestions of illusionism take precedence, Metsu's image gained inspiration from a series of artistic and intellectual contexts in the seventeenth century. *Woman Reading a Book by a Window* also offered a challenge to these traditions, transcending the spaces of male scholarship and expanding the possibilities of an inner world, now made large before our eyes.

NOTES

This essay has benefited from stimulating conversations with Laura Thiel-Convery and Amanda Capern, as well as thoughtful suggestions from Arthur K. Wheelock Jr.

1   For Metsu's early career and biography, see Adriaan E. Waiboer, "The Early Years of Gabriel Metsu," *Burlington Magazine* 147 (2005): 80–90.

2   Adriaan E. Waiboer, *Gabriel Metsu, Life and World: A Catalogue Raisonné* (New Haven, CT: Yale University Press, 2012), 26–27, 171, no. A14; and Adriaan E. Waiboer, "Woman Reading a Book by a Window" (2017), in *The Leiden Collection Catalogue*, 3rd ed., ed. Arthur K. Wheelock Jr. and Lara Yeager-Crasselt, 2020–, http://www.theleidencollection.com/artwork/a-woman-reading -a-letter-by-a-window/.

3   Scholarship was understood to be a male vocation. Although the reality was somewhat different (see discussion below), images of women engaged in scholarly activity are rare. An exception, attributed to the Monogrammist IS, is *Reading Woman in a Study*, ca. 1633–58 (Müller Collection, Staatliches Museum Schwerin, Germany). For the subject of women reading without the trappings of the scholarly study, see Gerard ter Borch the Elder, *Portrait of a Girl Reading*, pen in brown ink and red chalk, ca. 1630–35 (Rijksmuseum, Amsterdam); Bartholomeus van der Helst, *Woman with a Book*, 1665, oil on canvas (Magnin Museum, Dijon, France); and Eglon van der Neer, *The Reader*, ca. 1660s, oil on canvas (Metropolitan Museum of Art, New York). Precedents to this subject matter are a group of paintings of old women reading executed by Jan Lievens, Rembrandt van Rijn, and Gerrit Dou in 1620s and early 1630s. These works focus on the piety of the elderly women, who are shown intensely read- ing religious texts and have often been interpreted as prophet- esses. See Lievens, *Old Woman Reading*, ca. 1621–23, oil on panel (Philadelphia Museum of Art); Rembrandt, *Old Woman Reading, Probably the Prophetess Anna*, 1631, oil on panel (Rijksmuseum, Amsterdam); and Dou, *Old Woman Reading*, ca. 1631–32, oil on canvas (Rijksmuseum, Amsterdam).

4   Notably, her velvet bonnet shares the conventions of academic dress at Leiden University. In 1631, the statutes of the university still stipulated wearing the velvet bonnet as part of the ceremony conferring the doctoral degree. See Marieke de Winkel, *Fashion and Fancy: Dress and Meaning in Rembrandt's Paintings* (Amsterdam: Amsterdam University Press, 2006), 62.

FIG. 2.5. Jan Jacobsz Wielant after Hendrick Rochusz van Dagen, *Scholar in His Chamber*, 1655–1714, engraving, 12 ⅛ × 8 ⅛ in. (30.9 × 20.6 cm). Rijksmuseum, Amsterdam, RP-P-1998-435.

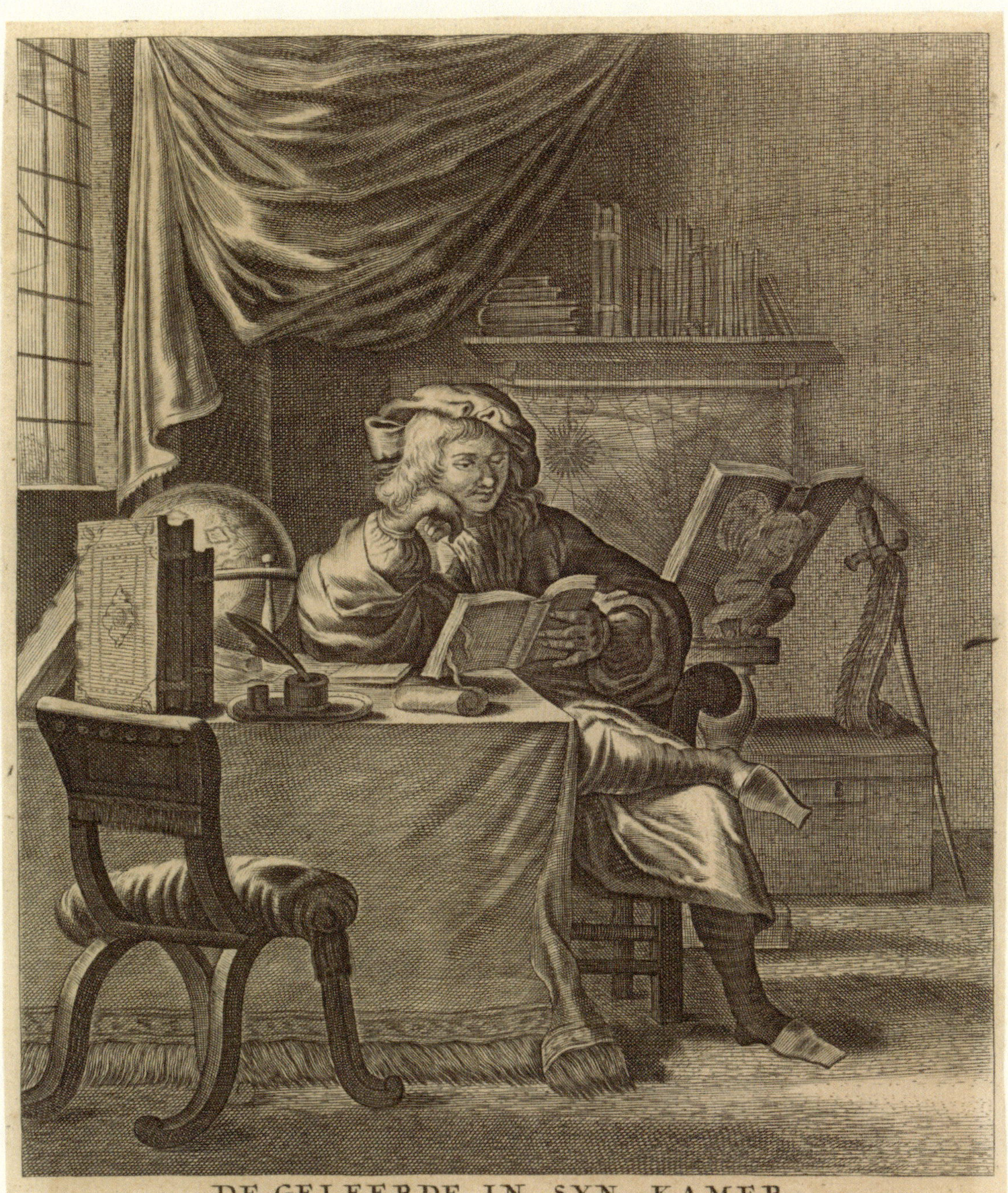

DE GELEERDE IN SYN KAMER

J. W. sculpsit   Lud. Nondius

5   My exploration of "an inner world" overlaps and intersects with the subject matter of figures engaged in the activities of reading and writing, as well as the pictorial tradition of the scholar at work. At the same time, it seeks to investigate this subject matter and its cultural associations more broadly. Important studies on these various themes include: Sabine Schulze, ed., *Leselust: niederländische Malerei von Rembrandt bis Vermeer* (Frankfurt am Main: Schirn Kunsthalle Frankfurt, 1993); Volker Manuth et al., *Wisdom, Knowledge and Magic: The Image of the Scholar in Seventeenth-Century Dutch Art* (Kingston, ON: Agnes Etherington Art Centre, 1996); Peter C. Sutton et al., *Love Letters: Dutch Genre Paintings in the Age of Vermeer* (Greenwich, CT: Bruce Museum of Arts and Science, 2004); Laura E. Thiel-Convery, "The Gentleman-Scholar at Home: Domesticity, Masculinity, and Civility in Dutch Seventeenth-Century Genre Painting," PhD diss., Queen's University, 2016; Adriaan E. Waiboer, Arthur K. Wheelock Jr., and Blaise Ducos, eds., *Vermeer and the Masters of Dutch Genre Painting* (New Haven, CT: Yale University Press, 2017), passim; and Laura E. Thiel-Convery and Wayne Franits, "'Keine Mühe der Welt gleicht dem Studium': Rembrandt und die Bildkonvention des Gelehrten in der niederländischen Genremalerei," in *Inside Rembrandt 1606–1669*, ed. Anja K. Sevcik (Cologne: Wallraf-Richartz-Museum & Fondation Corboud; Petersberg: Michael Imhof Verlag, 2019), 29–42.

6   Although this subject matter was not limited to artists working in Leiden, the number of images related to these themes produced there indicates that there was a considerable interest in such scenes on the part of both artists and collectors. The impact of Leiden as a university city has been widely noted by scholars, but it has not been examined in a cohesive way, with discussions largely focused around Rembrandt and his circle. See, for example, Mariët Westermann, "Making a Mark in Rembrandt's Leiden," in *Rembrandt Creates Rembrandt: Art and Ambition in Leiden, 1629–1631*, ed. Alan Chong (Boston: Isabella Stewart Gardner Museum, 2000), 25–49; and Jacquelyn Coutré, "Rembrandus Hermanni Leydensis: Rembrandt, Son of Harmen, of Leiden," in *Rembrandt Emerges: Leiden Circa 1630*, ed. Jacquelyn Coutré (Kingston, ON: Agnes Etherington Art Centre, 2019), 20–25.

7   A notable exception to the tradition of "fine painting" in this exhibition is Metsu's *Woman Reading a Book by a Window*. Metsu adapted this scholarly subject matter in a large-scale format and departed from the style of the *fijnschilders* in his broad and loose handling of brushwork. While Metsu later adopted a more "fine" manner of painting after his move to Amsterdam, the tension that he created in this work between subject matter and style reflects the painting's distinctive visual and thematic richness. For a discussion of issues of illusionism in the work of Dou, see Angela Ho, "Gerrit Dou's Enchanting Trompe l'Oeil: Virtuosity and Agency in Early Modern Collections," *Journal of Historians of Netherlandish Art* 7:1 (Winter 2015), DOI: 10.5092/jhna.2015.7.1.1.

8   Jan Orlers, *Beschrijvinge der Stad Leyden* (Leiden, 1641), 378.

9   The scholarship on Gerrit Dou and the Leiden fine painters is vast. See Eric Jan Sluijter, "Schilders van 'cleyne, subtile ende curieuse dingen': Leidse fijnschilders in contemporaine bronnen," in *Leidse Fijnschilders: van Gerrit Dou tot Frans van Mieris de Jonge, 1630–1760*, ed. Eric Jan Sluijter, Marlies Enklaar, and Paul Nieuwenhuizen, exh. cat. (Leiden: Museum De Lakenhal; Zwolle: Waanders, 1988), 36–46; Eric Jan Sluijter, "On Fijnschilders and Meaning," in *Seductress of Sight: Studies in Dutch Art of the Golden Age* (Zwolle: Waanders, 2000), 265–95; and Ronni Baer, Arthur K. Wheelock Jr., and Annetje Boersma, *Gerrit Dou, 1613–1675: Master Painter in the Age of Rembrandt* (Washington, DC: National Gallery of Art, 2001). For more recent evaluations of the "brand" for *fijnschilders* and the art market, see Angelo Ho, *Creating Distinctions in Dutch Genre Painting: Repetition and Invention* (Amsterdam: Amsterdam University Press, 2017). While Dou, his renowned pupil Frans van Mieris, and Gabriel Metsu have been well studied, the other artists represented in this exhibition, who were active in the late seventeenth century, have received considerably less attention. A recent and important exception is Junko Aono, *Confronting the Golden Age: Imitation and Innovation in Dutch Genre Painting, 1680–1750* (Amsterdam: Amsterdam University Press, 2015).

10   For an overview of the founding of the university and its relationship to the city, see Anthony Grafton, "Civic Humanism and Scientific Scholarship at Leiden," in *The University and the City: From Medieval Origins to the Present*, ed. Thomas Bender (New York: Oxford University Press, 1988), 59–78; and Ingrid W. L. Moerman, "Leiden, City in Holland," appendix in *Young Rembrandt: The Leiden Years, 1606–1632*, Roelof van Straten (Leiden: Foelor Publishers, 2005), 241–46.

11   Students could learn an array of languages at the university as well, including Greek, Latin, Hebrew, and Arabic. Between 1626 and 1650, Leiden enrolled 11,000 students. Jonathan Israel, *The Dutch Republic: Its Rise, Greatness, and Fall 1477–1806* (Oxford: Clarendon Press, 2007), 572.

12   For Sylvius's patronage of Gerrit Dou and Frans van Mieris, see Eric Jan Sluijter, "'All Striving to adorne their houses with costly peeces': The Case Studies of Paintings in Wealthy Interiors," in *Art & Home: Dutch Interiors in the Age of Rembrandt*, ed. Mariët Westermann, exh. cat. (Denver: Denver Art Museum, 2001), 102–27; Piet Bakker, "Gerrit Dou and His Collectors in the Golden Age" (2017), in *The Leiden Collection Catalogue*, 3rd ed., ed. Arthur K. Wheelock and Lara Yeager-Crasselt, 2020–,

http://www.theleidencollection.com/essays/gerrit-dou-and-his
-collectors-in-the-golden-age/.

13 The library was officially founded in 1585 with donations from
faculty and Leiden residents. Its early volumes were primarily
religious in nature but grew to include classical texts and
linguistic studies. Moerman, "Leiden, City in Holland," 243.

14 Plantin's firm became the official university printer in 1583.
Plantin's son-in-law, Franciscus I Raphelengius (1539–1597),
a scholar-printer and professor at the university, subsequently
took over the firm with his sons until 1618. The longstanding
Elsevier publishing house succeeded the Leidse Officina
Plantiniana as university publisher. See E. van Gulik, "Drukkkers
en Geleerden. De leidse Officina Plantiniana (1583–1619),"
in *Leiden University in the Seventeenth Century: An Exchange of
Learning*, ed. Theodoor Herman Lunsingh Scheurleer and
G. H. M. Posthumus Meyjes (Leiden: Universitaire Pers Leiden,
1975), 368; and Paul Hoftijzer, "The Dutch Republic, Centre of
the European Book Trade in the 17th Century," *European History
Online* (EGO), published by the Leibniz Institute of European
History (IEG), Mainz, November 23, 2015, http://www.ieg-ego
.eu/hoftijzerp-2015-en. Jacquelyn Coutré notes that in 1725,
the Swiss doctor Albrecht van Haller observed how printers and
booksellers could be found everywhere in the city. See Coutré,
"Rembrandus Hermanni Leydensis," 34n43.

15 The Dutch population was generally well educated,
and many families sent their children at least to grammar
school. Boys could attend Latin school and then possibly
university, while girls were only permitted to continue their
studies in sewing school or a French school to learn etiquette.
See Hoftijzer, "The Dutch Republic." For an overview of literacy
in early modern Europe, see Robert A. Houston, "Literacy,"
European History Online (EGO), published by the Institute of
European History (IEG), Mainz, November 28, 2011,
http://www.ieg-ego.eu/houstonr-2011-en.

16 Houston, "Literacy."

17 The book still life also flourished in Leiden in the late 1620s
in the works of Jan Davidsz de Heem and Jan Lievens. For the
market for these paintings, see Piet Bakker, "Rembrandt and the
Emergence of the Leiden Art Market," in *Rembrandt Emerges:
Leiden Circa 1630*, ed. Jacquelyn Coutré (Kingston, ON:
Agnes Etherington Art Centre, 2019), 78.

18 Orlers's text documented the city's history, describing its ancient
Roman and medieval origins, its political and civic institutions,
and the founding of its renowned university. Like other local
historians, Orlers considered Leiden an ancient city because it
was believed to have served as the Roman fort of Lugdunum on
the *Tabula Peutigeriana*. Orlers went so far as to declare Leiden
Holland's oldest city: "Leiden [is] not just old but the oldest and
principal city of Holland, certainly older than Dordrecht and
Haarlem." As cited in Karl A. E. Enenkel and Konrad A.
Ottenheym, trans. Alexander C. Thomson, "The Mediaeval
Prestige of Dutch Cities," in *Ambitious Antiquities, Famous
Forebears: Constructions of a Glorious Past in the Early Modern
Netherlands and in Europe* (Leiden: Brill, 2019), 336.

19 The first edition of Orlers's text contained the lives of a
small number of famous painters, and by 1641, as the city had
blossomed into more of an artistic center, these biographies
expanded to include contemporary Leiden artists, among them
David Bailly, Joris van Schooten, Jan van Goyen, Rembrandt van
Rijn, Jan Lievens, and Gerrit Dou.

20 Orlers, as cited in Eric Jan Sluijter, "In Praise of the Art of
Painting: On Paintings by Gerrit Dou and a Treatise by Philips
Angel of 1642," in *Seductress of Sight: Studies in Dutch Art of
the Golden Age* (Zwolle: Waanders, 2000), 201.

21 See discussion in Sluijter, "In Praise of the Art of Painting," 201–3.
Sluijter notes that most other civic historians paid little attention
to contemporary painters.

22 Angel spoke on October 18, 1641, the feast day honoring St. Luke,
the patron saint of painters. There are various interpretations
of the aims of Angel's text, and whether or not it constituted a
theoretical treatise, but one motivating factor may have been
the painters' wish to establish a guild, which would not exist in
Leiden until 1648. See Hessel Miedema, "Philips Angels
'Lof der schilder-konst,'" *Oud Holland* 103, no. 4 (1989): 181–222;
and Sluijter, "In Praise of the Art of Painting," 198–263.

23 Angel, as cited in Sluijter, "In Praise of the Art of Painting," 207.

24 Minerva had been adopted as part of the university's shield
in 1581.

25 The word on the pedestal below—PICTURA—has replaced
AC(ademia) LUG(duno) BAT (ava). See Sluijter, "In Praise of
the Art of Painting," 207; and H. Perry Chapman, "A Hollandse
Pictura: Observations on the Title Page of Philips Angel's 'Lof
der schilder-konst,'" *Simiolus* 16, no. 4 (1986): 233–48.

26 Precedents to this subject matter include images of St. Jerome
as a scholar; see Susan Kuretsky, "Rembrandt's Tree Stump:
An Iconographic Attribute of St. Jerome," *Art Bulletin* 56 (1974):
571–80; and Catherine Scallen, "Rembrandt's Reformation on a
Catholic Subject: The Penitent and the Repentant Saint Jerome,"
Sixteenth-Century Journal 30 (1999): 71–88. For the tradition of
depicting saints in the act of writing, from St. Jerome to
substitutions of Jerome as Luther, see Shira Brisman,
"Privileged Mediators," in *Albrecht Dürer and the Epistolary
Mode of Address* (Chicago: University of Chicago Press, 2016),
109–30.

27 This marked a shift in emphasis from previous depictions of
the saints as martyrs.

28 Leiden was home to the first theological college in the
Netherlands, which was founded in 1592 as the Statencollege.
It attracted leading theologians in the first decade of the
seventeenth century, including the professors Jacobus Arminius
and Franciscus Gomarus, who held opposing views on the
subject of free will and predestination. The dispute between
the Remonstrants (Arminians) and the more orthodox Counter-
Remonstrants (Gomarists) erupted into violence in Leiden
between 1617 and 1621. These religious debates reverberated
throughout the United Provinces, but as Sir Dudley Carleton,
the English ambassador at The Hague, remarked in 1617,
Leiden was at "the fountain of these dissensions."
Dudley Carleton, *Letters from and to Sir Dudley Carleton,
Knt. during His Embassy in Holland from January 1616 to
December 1620*, as quoted in Israel, *The Dutch Republic*, 442.

29 In addition to secular images of scholars, Dou also repeatedly
depicted hermits—often accompanied by instruments of
scholarly pursuits. For a discussion of Dou's hermits, see Arthur K.
Wheelock Jr., "Gerrit Dou, *The Hermit*, 1670," *Dutch Paintings of
the Seventeenth Century*, NGA Online Editions, April 24, 2014,
http://purl.org/nga/collection/artobject/46032.

30 He is surrounded by the trappings of his profession: books,
writing instruments, a globe, as well as hourglasses and a skull,
which served as *vanitas* symbols referring to the passing of time
and a reminder of one's own mortality. For further discussion,
see Dominique Surh, "Scholar Interrupted at His Writing" (2017),
in *The Leiden Collection Catalogue*, 3rd ed., ed. Arthur K.
Wheelock Jr. and Lara Yeager-Crasselt, 2020–, http://www
.theleidencollection.com/artwork/a-scholar-interrupted
-at-his-writing/. The *tabbaard*, which originated as a fashionable
outer garment for men, had become outmoded by the seventeenth
century, yet it was still worn by members of the magistrate,
clergy, and university as a mark of *dignitas*, *gravitas*, and *studio*.
See De Winkel, *Fashion and Fancy*, 36–39.

31 The first book of scholarly portraits appeared in 1609 (*Icones*),
followed by the *Illustris Academia* (1613), *Alma Academia* (1614),
Icones elogia ac vitae (1617), and *Athenae Batavae* (1625).
See Marijke Tolsma, "Van icons tot effigies: de in 1609 in
boekvorm uitgegeven portrettencollectie van Leidse geleerden
en haar navolgers," PhD diss., Leiden University, 2016.

32 The books were collected early on by a small intellectual and
elite audience in Leiden, while later editions became souvenirs
for those who had either attended or visited the university.
Tolsma, "Van icons tot effigies."

33 Dou may have gained inspiration from Rembrandt's *Portrait of
a Scholar*, 1631 (State Hermitage Museum, St. Petersburg), or
the etching of *Jan Uytenbogaert*, 1635, both of which show men
interrupted from writing and reading, respectively.

34 Ann Jensen Adams discusses this concept in regard to Dutch
portraiture. See Adams, "Temporality and the Seventeenth-
Century Dutch Portrait," in *Journal of Historians of Netherlandish
Art* 5, no. 2 (Summer 2013), DOI: 10.5092/jhna.2013.5.2.15.

35 Simon van Leeuwen published his history of Leiden in
1672. Simon van Leeuwen, *Korte besgryving van het Lugdunum
Batavorum nu Leyden* (Leiden, 1672), 191–92. See also
Henriette Rahusen, "Portrait of a Man Reading a Book" (2017),
in *The Leiden Collection Catalogue*, 3rd ed., ed. Arthur K.
Wheelock Jr. and Lara Yeager-Crasselt, 2020–, http://www
.theleidencollection.com/artwork/portrait-of-a-man-reading-a
-book/.

36 The *Japonse rock* became fashionable around midcentury,
and gradually replaced the *tabbaard* as a fashion associated with
learning and prestige. See De Winkel, *Fashion and Fancy*, 36–39;
and Martha Hollander, "Vermeer's Robe: Costume, Commerce,
and Fantasy in the Early Modern Netherlands," *Dutch Crossing:
Journal of Low Countries Studies* 35 (2011): 177–95.

37 Toorenvliet's painting presents a positive image of alchemy in
contrast to the negative pictorial tradition that followed Pieter
Brueghel the Elder's drawing *The Alchemist*, engraved by Philips
Galle, ca. 1558. See Elisabeth Berry Drago, *Painted Alchemists:
Early Modern Artistry and Experiment in the Work of Thomas
Wijck* (Amsterdam: Amsterdam University Press, 2019),
especially 27–57.

38 The secrecy involved in the alchemist's profession is discussed
in Drago, *Painted Alchemists*, 29–37.

39 See Adriaan E. Waiboer, "Public Notary" (2017), in *The Leiden
Collection Catalogue*, 3rd ed., ed. Arthur K. Wheelock Jr. and
Lara Yeager-Crasselt, 2020–, http://www.theleidencollection
.com/artwork/a-public-notary/.

40 Dou developed this motif in the 1640s. For discussion of the
motif and further bibliography, see Angela Ho, "A Niche of
One's Own: Gerrit Dou's Brand-Building Project," in *Creating
Distinctions in Dutch Genre Painting: Repetition and Invention*
(Amsterdam: Amsterdam University Press, 2002), 53–92.

41 See Ho, "A Niche of One's Own," especially 61–67.

42 Solitude was seen as essential for serious intellectual endeavor,
a concept that derives from precedents like Saint Jerome in
the wilderness or in his study. For example, see Willem van
Mieris's painting *Hermit Praying in the Wilderness* (cat. 6).
See Thiel-Convery and Franits, "'Keine Mühe der Welt,'" 31.

43 See Eddy de Jongh and Ger Luijten, *Mirror of Everyday Life:
Genreprints in the Netherlands 1550–1700* (Amsterdam:
Rijksmuseum, 1997), 329–32.

44 I would like to thank Laura Thiel-Convery for bringing
this reference and the print by Van Dagen to my attention.
Machiavelli's letter was written in 1513 to Francesco Vettori.

He begins by describing how he was "compelled to change from his everyday clothes into robes of academia before stepping foot in his study." See J. R. Hale, ed. and trans., *The Literary Works of Machiavelli* (London: Oxford University Press, 1961), 139.

45 See note 3.

46 See Waiboer, "Woman Reading a Book by a Window."

47 Cesare Ripa, *Iconologia, of uytbeeldingen des verstands [. . .]*, trans. Dirck P. Pers (Amsterdam, 1644), 273. A nearly identical image of this female figure appears in the eighteenth-century edition of Ripa included in this exhibition (cat. 17) and illustrated on the back cover. Similarly seated before a book with an outstretched hand and holding a torch, this elegant personification of *Cognizione* also receives illumination from an open window behind her.

48 See Waiboer, "Woman Reading a Book by a Window." For the symbolic role of light as intellectual and spiritual illumination, see Thiel-Convery and Franits, "'Keine Mühe der Welt,'" 36–37.

49 Metsu was probably in Utrecht around 1650–51 before returning to Leiden for several years. He left for Amsterdam permanently in 1654–55. For discussion of Metsu's stay in Utrecht, see Adriaan E. Waiboer, "The Early Years of Gabriel Metsu," *Burlington Magazine* 147 (2005): 83–89.

50 Van Schurman was permitted to attend lectures at the University of Utrecht, which had been founded in 1636. See Joyce L. Irwin, "Anna Maria van Schurman and Her Intellectual Circle," in Anna Maria van Schurman, *Whether a Christian Woman Should Be Educated and Other Writings from Her Intellectual Circle*, ed. and trans. Joyce L. Irwin (Chicago: University of Chicago Press, 1998); Pieta van Beek, *The First Female University Student: Anna Maria van Schurman* (1636) (Utrecht: Igitur, 2010); and Arthur K. Wheelock Jr., "Nothing Gray about Her: Cornelis Jonson van Ceulen's Grisaille of Anna Maria van Schurman," in *Facebook: Studies on Dutch and Flemish Portraiture of the 16th–18th centuries*, ed. Edwin Buijsen, Charles Dumas, and Volker Manuth (Leiden: Primavera, 2012), 325–30.

51 Pieta van Beek notes that this was not a dissertation in the modern sense of the word, but rather a demonstration of logical argumentation *(Dissertatio)*. Van Beek, *First Female University Student*, 65.

52 See Amanda L. Capern, "Literature and Letters," in *The Routledge History of Women in Early Modern Europe*, ed. Amanda L. Capern (London: Routledge, 2019), 416; and Arthur K. Wheelock Jr., "Cornelis Jonson van Ceulen, *Anna Maria van Schurman, 1657*," *Dutch Paintings of the Seventeenth Century*, NGA Online Editions, April 24, 2014, http://purl.org/nga/collection /artobject/123073.

53 Capern, "Literature and Letters," 416. Van Schurman was also recognized for her artistic talents and granted entry in Utrecht's

Guild of St. Luke in 1643. See Katlijne Van der Stighelen, "'Et ses artistes mains . . .' The Art of Anna Maria van Schurman," in *Choosing the Better Part: Anna Maria van Schurman* (1607–1678), ed. M. De Baar et al. (Dordrecht: Kluwer Academic Publishers, 1996), 58.

54 My thanks to Arthur K. Wheelock Jr. for making this suggestion.

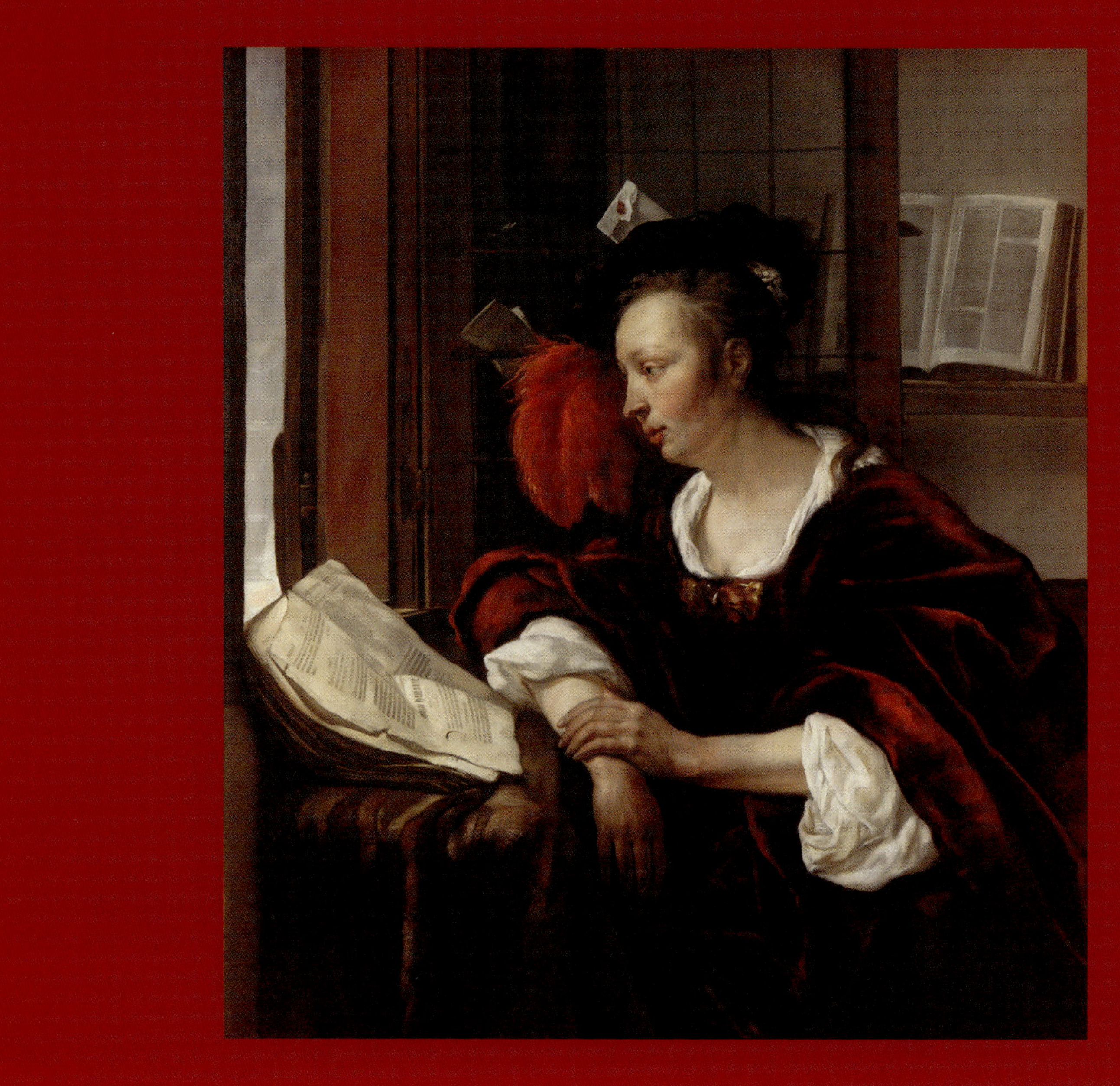

Private Life and Public Record in Two Paintings by Gabriel Metsu

Shira Brisman

Gabriel Metsu, *Woman Reading a Book by a Window*, ca. 1653–54, oil on canvas, 41 5/16 × 35 3/4 in. (105 × 90.7 cm). The Leiden Collection, New York.

Gabriel Metsu, *Public Notary*, ca. 165(3?), oil on panel, 16 1/8 × 12 13/16 in. (41 × 32.5 cm). The Leiden Collection, New York.

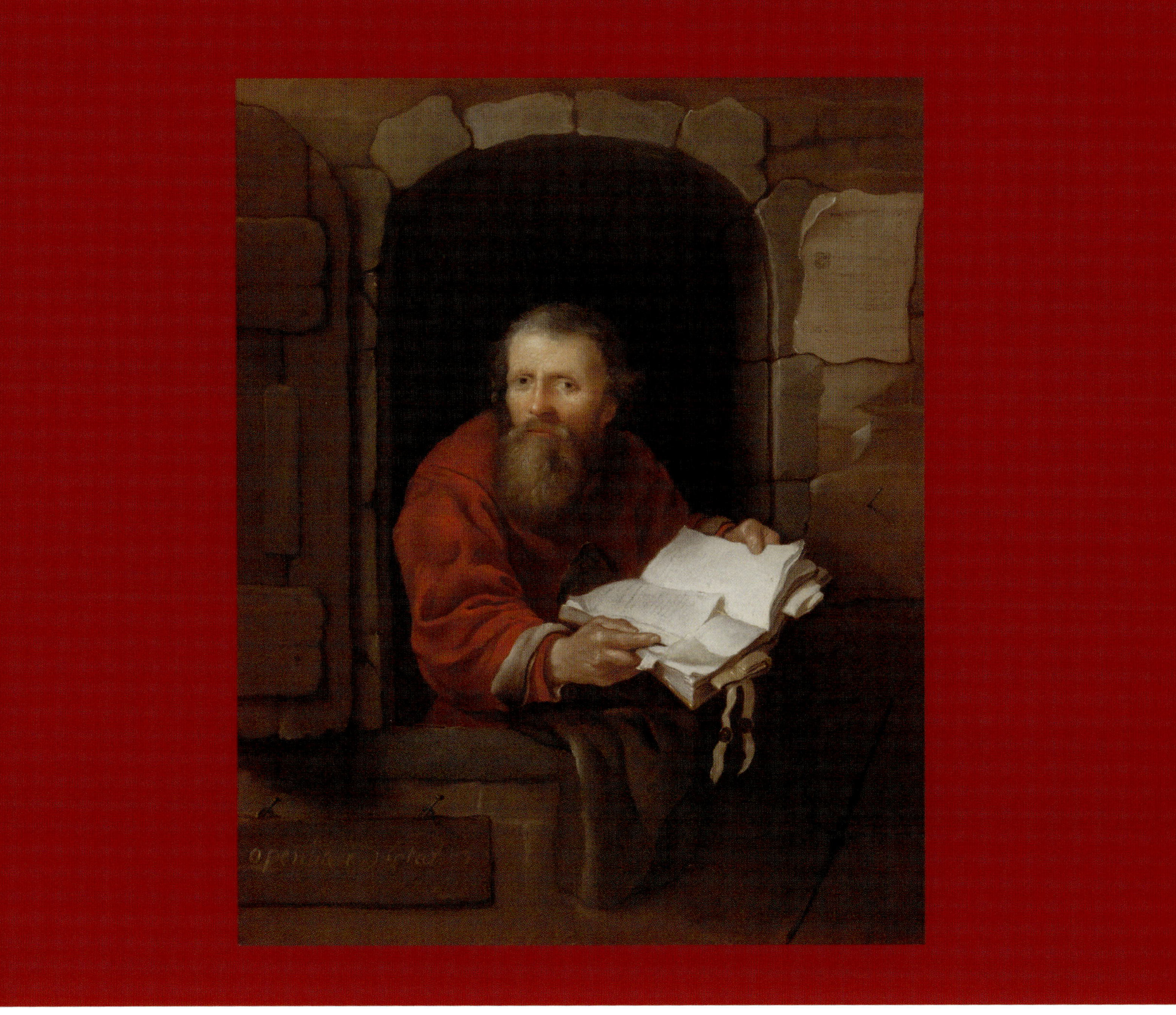

I n two paintings dating to the mid-1650s by Gabriel Metsu (1629–1667), windows mediate between private and public spaces, as do wax seals. *Woman Reading a Book by a Window* (cat. 4) situates the beholder in the same interior as the subject, who is presented in profile, her head backed by an open windowpane that also serves as a letter rack. One missive bears the signature of the painter; the other is tucked over, its red seal promising to protect what is written inside. Metsu's *Public Notary* (cat. 3) confronts the viewer directly by leaning out the window.[1] He holds a notebook, out of which peeks a folded document with two hanging seals. These authenticating marks indicate the more public function of the paper to which they are attached, as opposed to the intimate correspondence the woman has received. The motifs of windows and seals in Metsu's two paintings point to how mid-seventeenth-century Dutch artists developed distinctive pictorial vocabularies for addressing their audiences alternately as possessors of rich inner lives or as participants in the civic order. The figuration of interiors and interiority for which the painting of this period is famous developed out of a culture that was becoming increasingly adept at registering the individual—that is, the male individual—as a member of the social world.

Looking up from her reading, leaning toward the light, the recipient of the sealed message in Metsu's painting has largely thrown off the trappings of the most famous female subject in Western art who shares with her those conditions. Though faint echoes of the Annunciation may remain—in one of its iconographic traditions, the angel Gabriel delivers the divine message in the form of a sealed document—Metsu's woman is no Virgin Mary.[2] Yet determining who she is makes for no easy task. Her hat and robe do not identify her as a contemporary woman from the mid-1650s; they are not what one would have worn while sitting at home.[3] If she is meant to evoke the mythological figure of Minerva, a connection to the insignia of Leiden University that Lara Yeager-Crasselt's essay in this catalogue explores, she appears here with only a limited number of the goddess's attributes. Absent are her helmet and shield—symbols of bellicosity that in other paintings help identify her, even when she has laid them aside to welcome more introspective epistemological pursuits.[4] If Metsu's woman stands more generally for the allegorical figure of Knowledge, as both Yeager-Crasselt and Adriaan E. Waiboer suggest, her wisdom encompasses not only information obtained through the reading of books but also insight gained through personal correspondence.[5] She may be an allegory, yet she is anything but a stiff conveyor of an abstract ideal. The reds of the wax seal, the feathered flourish of the woman's cap, and the rosiness of her cheeks connect through color her secrets, her affectations, and her desires.[6]

Letters are communications that have traveled a distance. As Dutch involvement in oceanic trade and its colonizing ambitions left wives uncertain and at home,[7] seventeenth-century painting positioned women in interiors reading dispatches from afar to evoke, through his absence, the adventurer and entrepreneur. Such a dynamic between sender and recipient structures the companion pieces that Metsu would later paint after his move to Amsterdam, *Man Writing a Letter* and *Woman Reading a Letter with a Maidservant* (FIGS. 3.1 and 3.2).[8] In the latter panel, a maidservant draws back the curtain from a painting of a ship while her mistress leans toward the light to read what her correspondent has written. But in the earlier *Woman Reading* painted in Leiden, both the correspondent and the subject of the woman's yearning must be imagined. She may look out the window longing for another's return or desiring to gain experience herself, to be out in the world.

Metsu's signature on the letter by her head is not to be mistaken for an indication that he has written to her, but rather signals that he has written to us, making an analogy between the painting and the missive. More substantial than the *cartellini* in Italian pictures, like those of Giovanni Bellini (1431/36–1516), where slips of paper attach to the surface of the image with a delicate nonfixity as if they might flutter away in the breeze, letters, protected by folds and seals, harbor hidden messages.[9] The letter softens the edges of allegory, pulling the painting into the domestic territory of genre scenes and setting at stake "the work's complex readability" by blurring the boundaries of categorization, inviting—and then blushingly denying—a hermeneutic process associated with the decoding of text.[10] The analogy between letters that shy away from legibility and the coyness of pictorial meaning permitted paintings of women in interiors reading letters to appeal to (male) beholders as occasions for contemplative reflection. These paintings offered a possibility for an existential condition that a marine mercantile economy otherwise did not promote: an association between being in touch with one's inner self and being at home. Bryan Wolf's book on paintings of women who read letters indoors explores the cartesian context of this gendered theme. A philosophy of the mind "requires, to return to our metaphor of the window, that we stay indoors . . . where we can examine our habits of thought beyond their instrumental uses." For artists like Johannes Vermeer (1632–1675), Pieter de Hooch (1629–1684), and Gabriel Metsu, Wolf continues, "painting and feminization go hand in hand: not because the artist and women share the same social and architectural spaces (though they often do), but because they share the same sorts of power: covert, implicit, and nonjuridical."[11]

This last point, that the woman wields control through furtive means but not by legal authority, contrasts her with the notary, who was not only the maker of public record but endowed with the authority to label paintings into what Mieke Bal has called "mastercodes"—that is, categories that direct the viewer to approach a work with a set of predetermined associations that establish the ground for the attribution of meaning.[12] The woman, whose thoughts remain obscure, with the help of the folded letters withdraws the indicators of her identity from the world. The notary, on the other hand, emerges as a namer of things. The task of classifying paintings by subject matter was one undertaken in the seventeenth century by a member of this profession who arrived at a home upon the death of an individual to take stock of an estate. Paintings were listed and sold at auction, sometimes through the *Weeskamer* (orphan chamber) or the *desolate Boedelkamer* (bankruptcy chamber). The notary was an early form of cataloguer whose ordering of paintings under rubrics of landscape, perspective, and portraiture omitted the name of the sitter or the precise mythological or biblical scene. Temporal distance drives the historian's desire to have more specific information. The modern convention of titling pictures is the eventual outcome of a transactional economy that had severed the direct connection between patron and maker. The speculative art market, one that needed to solicit the attention of a potential buyer, would eventually also engage that buyer as a critic by providing a painting with a name by which to evaluate image against word.[13] In its day, however, a seventeenth-century painting did not require such precise description for successful immediate resale. John Michael Montias has called the standardization of a limited vocabulary for paintings on the art market a "public good" that facilitates recognition and communication.[14] The notary enabled the expeditious transfer of paintings from old home to new.

The notary's task, more broadly speaking, was to record an individual's belongings, speeches, and acts for the purpose of registering the existence of that individual as part of the public. He ensured trust in civil society by guaranteeing the integrity of private transactions.[15] In other words (and at the risk of glorifying the bureaucrat), his job was to make people count. A statement signed by a notary indicated that it was "true in law"; it was a document that conceived of a future audience to whom it delivers a testimony: "Notarial records are in this sense always in implicit dialogue with an imagined litigious future."[16] This point, which has been made in recent scholarship by Kathryn Burns, was also made more wryly in a sixteenth-century print from the series *Litis abusus (The Abuses of the Law)* (FIG. 3.3). Here, a notary, blindfolded to indicate his ignorance, records the deal of two merchants, whose hands are being forced together by the personifications *Falsitas* (Deceit) and *Fraus* (Fraud). The text below reads: "Door t'scalke bedroch, door valscheit argelistich/ooc door scryvers zot werdt de coopman meest twistich" (Through devious fraud, through deceitful falsehood, and also through foolish scribes has the merchant become most litigious). This scene, engraved by Hendrick Goltzius (1558–1617), was conceived by Dirck Volckertsz Coornhert (1522–1590), a scholar and engraver who was himself also notary.[17]

In addition to inventorying property, the notary served as an official witness, his signature verifying an orally

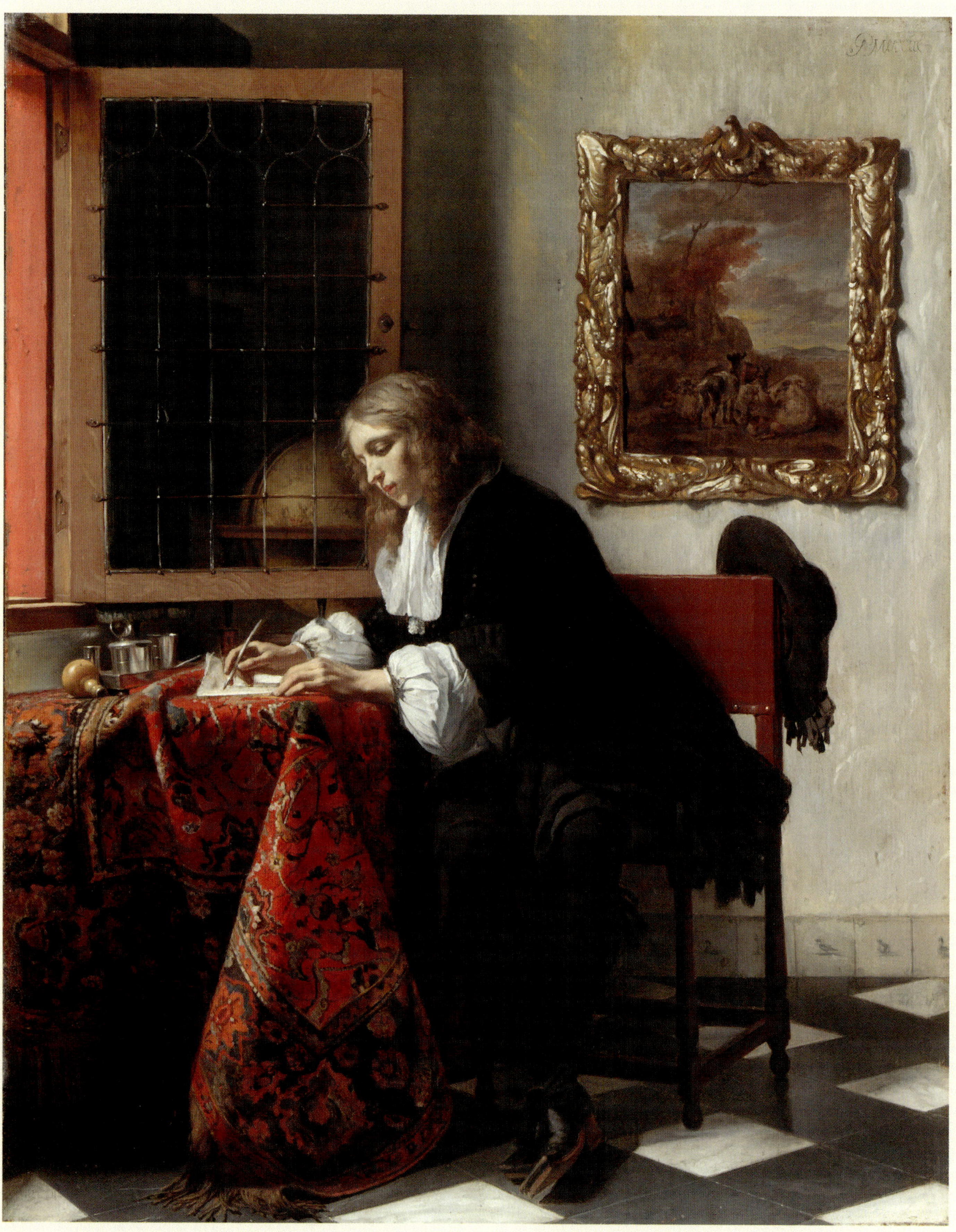

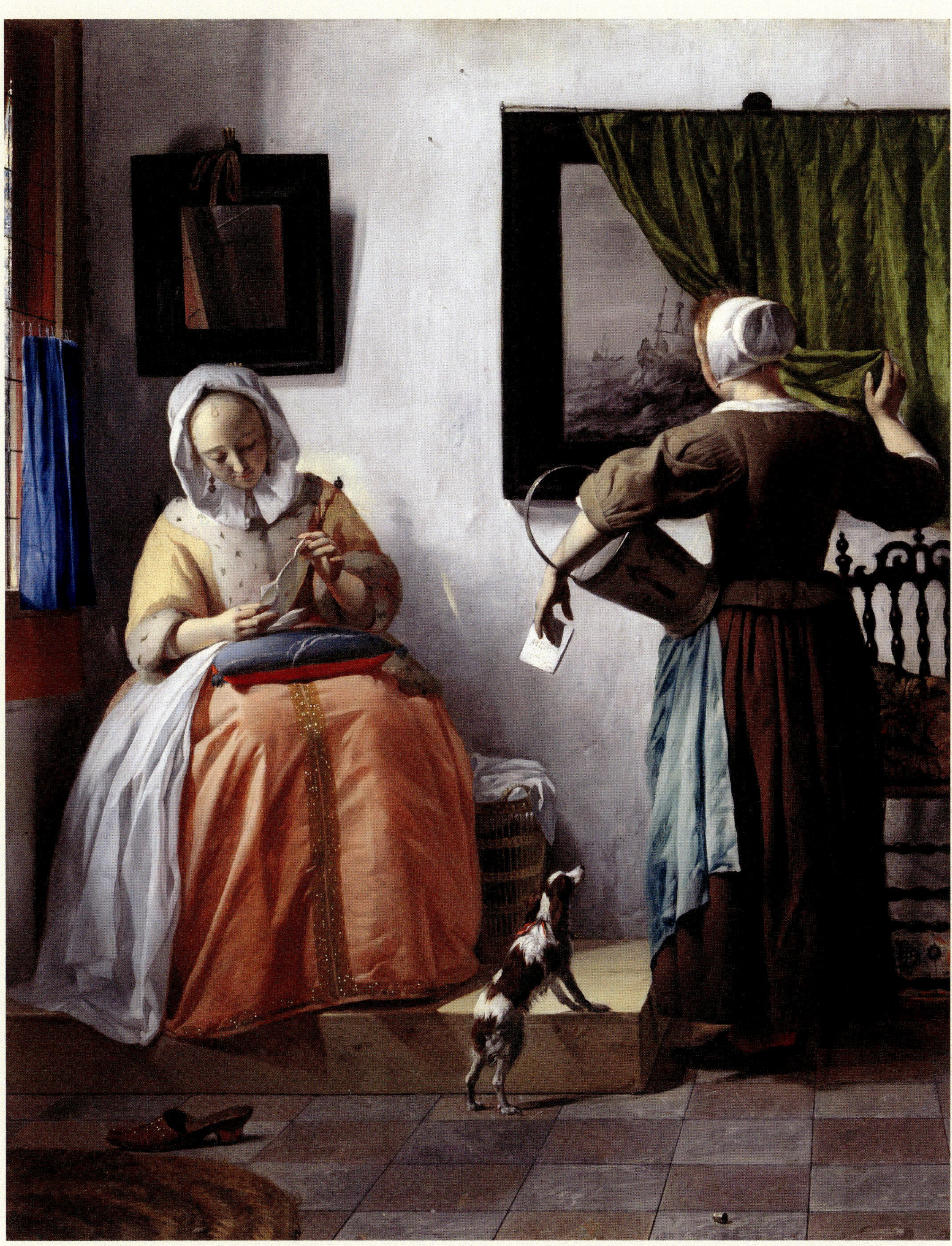

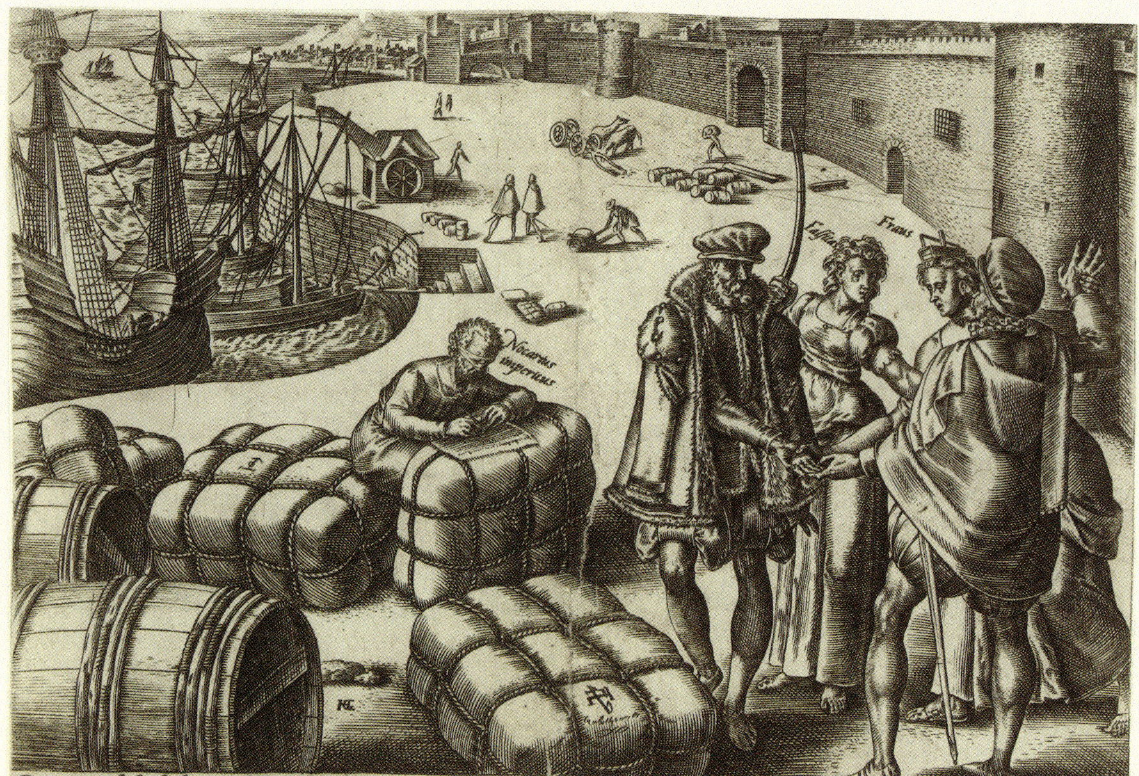

Door escalke bedroch, door valscheit argelistich,
Sed vos iniuriam facitis et fraudatis: et hoc fribus. i.Cor. 6. Ne fraudem feceris. Mar.10.
Abominatio est apud Dñm pondus et pondus, statera dolosa non est bona. Pro.20.
Malum est, malü est. dicit omnis emptor: et cum recesserit, tunc gloriabitur. Pro.20.
Oia ergo quæcunq vultis ut faciant vobis homines: et vos facite illis. Matth. 7.
2. ooc door scryuers zot werdt de Coopman meest twistich.
Sunder ir thud unrecht, und verforteilen, und folichs an den brüderen _. j.Corint.6.
Dem Herren ists ein greuwel zweierley gewicht, und ein falsce wag ist ein bösz ding.
Es ist bösz, es ist bösz, spricht der, der etwas kauft: so es aber im wirt so lobt ers. Prou.20
Allesmin das ir wöllend dz euch die leut thün sollend, dasz thünd euch ir inen. Matth. 7.

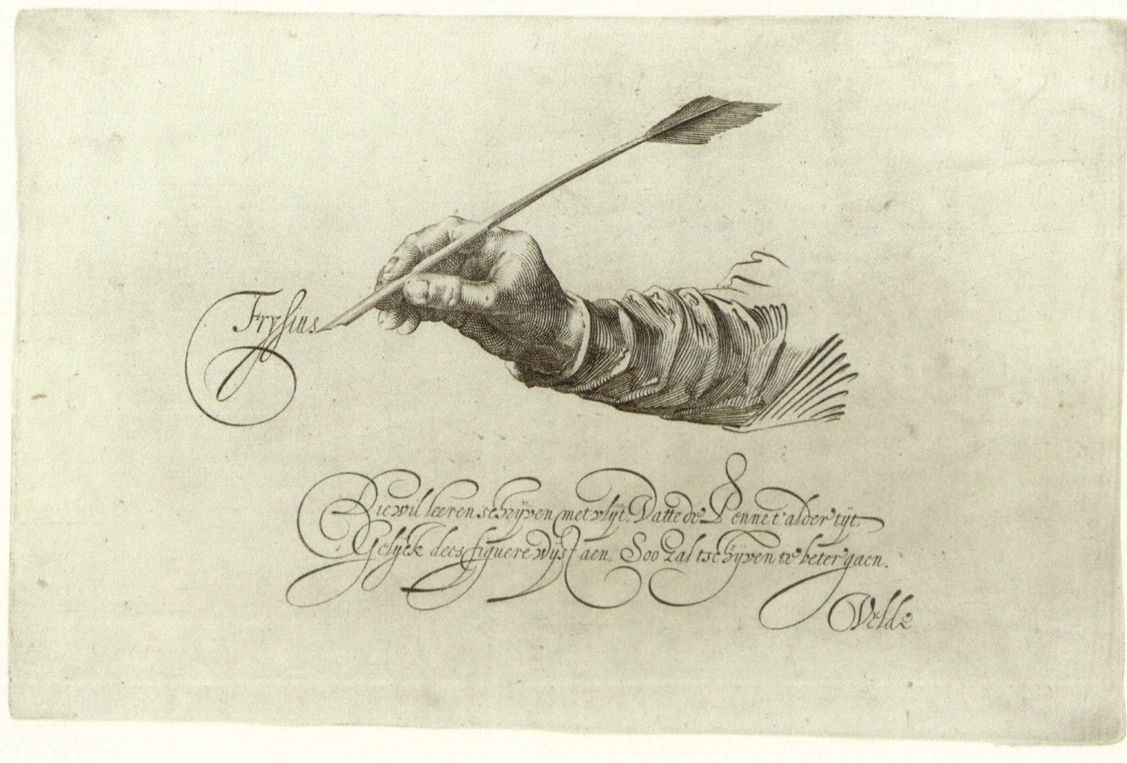

Fryfius
Die wil leeren schrijven met vlijt, Datte de Penne t'alder tijt.
Gelijck dees figuere wijst aen, Soo zal tschrijven u beter gaen.
Velde

delivered testimony. For this reason, the notary's records are vital to the historian's work. For example, we know the location of Gabriel Metsu's home in 1657 along the Prinsengracht canal in Amsterdam because of a notary's record that presents his neighbor's testimony affirming his claim that someone was stealing his chickens.[18] Metsu himself appears in the Amsterdam notarial records as witness, in 1660, when he is called upon to verify the duration of residence of two women who lived at an address nearby to him.[19] In 1643 and 1645, while still a citizen of Leiden, he had likewise acted as witness to events concerning his neighborhood.[20] These archives account not only for the painter's whereabouts but also for a sense of local community that constitutes its public identity through the requirement of affirmations of interpersonal relationships in the form of official records.

While the notary was an office that traced back to the Roman Republic, his training and influence was circumscribed by his jurisdiction. He wrote in the vernacular and in a regional style. The *Spieghel der schrijfkonste* (*Mirror of the Art of Writing*), a calligraphic manual engraved by Simon Frisius (ca. 1580–1629) based on *modelli* supplied by Jan van de Velde (1593–1641), demonstrates the differences in the loops and swirls between Dutch, German, French, and English notarial methods (FIG. 3.4).[21] Van de Velde crafts his analysis of the *Nederlandtsche principale gemeyne handen* (principles of the Netherlandish common hand) with a political bite: he counsels against incorporating Spanish and Italian bastardizations into Dutch cursive in order to preserve the graceful oscillations of thick to thin in the lively, local hand.[22] The allegiances of the notary are also reflected in

the oath he swore when assuming office. By the late sixteenth century, this was no longer to the monarch but to the provincial state.[23]

In Metsu's painting, the notary holds a thick journal of papers, but the only legible writing is the statement of his profession on the board that hangs below the window—*openbaer Notarus*.[24] Below this, Metsu has given the date, 1655.[25] The sign operates with self-reflexivity; it is a form of pictorial writing within the picture that gives information about the picture itself. The metadata here is different from the metadata of the signature that appears on the folded letter in *Woman Reading a Book by a Window*. There, the hidden message of the correspondence honors an alignment between painting and suppression of speech. *Stilswijgentheyt* (silence), according to the writing of Karel van Mander, gives birth to the pictorial sign; it endows visual form with meaning.[26] Van Mander praised letters as *stomme boden* (silent messengers).[27] The letters within Metsu's *Woman Reading* signal silence through their closure. Seals of letters are like lips; they open and shut. The color of their wax can lend an erotic blush to white paper, as lips do to a face. Metsu's painting of the notary, on the other hand, does not offer symbols of silence. It solicits speech. It advertises the availability of a public witness, one who is ready to make official record of a pronouncement. His office grants him the authority to bring words into being.

Painting—especially Northern European painting—has often operated under the fantasy that it can take on the authority of a notarial document. This fantasy has long been shared by historians of art, as best exemplified by an essay by Erwin Panofsky from 1934,

FIG. 3.3. Hendrick Goltzius, *The Ignorant Notary* from the series *Litis abusus* (*The Abuses of the Law*), 1597, engraving, 6 ½ × 8 ¹³⁄₁₆ in. (16.6 × 22.4 cm). Rijksprentenkabinet, Rijksmuseum, Amsterdam, RP-P-OB-10.262.

FIG. 3.4. Jan van den Velde, *Pen-Hold for the Netherlandish Hand*, from Part I of the *Spieghel der schrijfkonste* (*Mirror of the Art of Writing*), 1605, engraving by Simon Frisius, 8 ⅝ × 13 ⅜ in. (22 × 33.9 cm). Rijksprentenkabinet, Rijksmuseum, Amsterdam, RP-P-1964-2117.

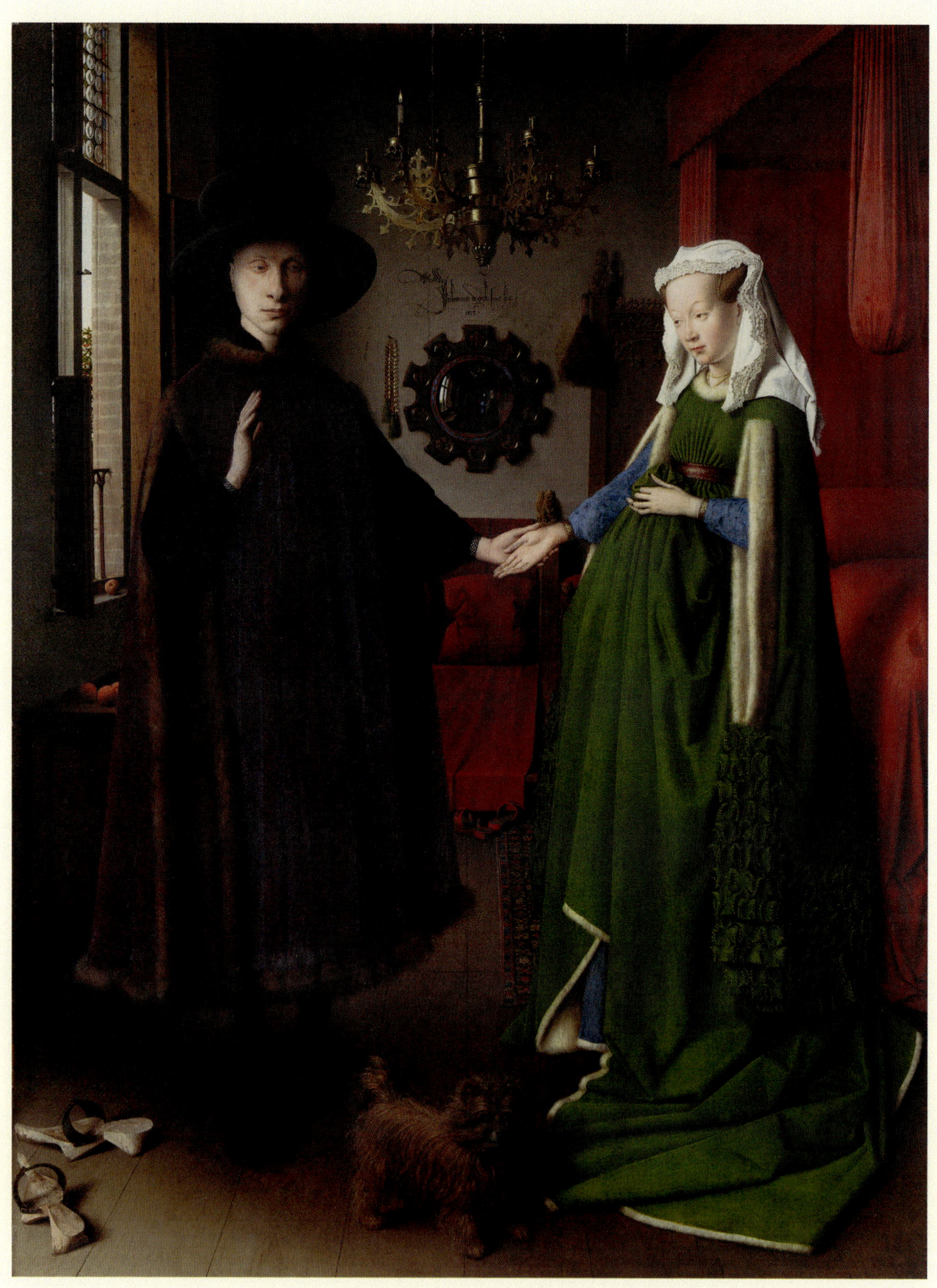

in which he imagines that Jan van Eyck's signature on the Arnolfini wedding (FIG. 3.5) acts as his witness statement to the marriage of the merchant and his wife. Panofsky saw the double portrait also as "a document at the same time," "a 'pictorial marriage certificate' in which the statement that 'Jan van Eyck had been there' had the same importance and implied the same legal consequences as an 'affidavit' deposed by a witness at a modern registrar's office."[28] Panofsky's theory has since been disproven by Margaret Koster's clarification that by the time of the date on the painting, 1434, Giovanni Arnolfini's wife had died.[29] If Van Eyck's signature records his witnessing of anything over the course of the commission, it was not a wedding but Costanza's departure.

Panofsky may have gotten the facts of the Arnolfini biography wrong, but did he not get something about the ambition of the painting right? It is the painting, even more than the painter Jan van Eyck, that wishes to bear witness to the marital oath taking place.[30] In other words, the painting's aim is to record a gesture of the hand and an utterance of the mouth that bring about a transformation of state. Marriages call for witnesses and seals because they are matters of public interest. They entail a transfer of property that is of import to a community beyond the two people who are joined. At the same time that painting was discovering that it could earn new significance by appealing to individual consciousness, drawing the beholder inside by indicating pictorially the privacy of thought, it was also considering how it might earn significance in the public sphere. It did this not only by establishing itself as property to be taken into the home but by envisioning what those interiors looked like, through a preponderance of domestic views— including Metsu's *Woman Reading a Book by a Window*. Seventeenth-century Dutch painting also solicited from its audience a pronouncement that could be of consequence in the social world. It is for this reason that Metsu's notary leans out of the window, addressing the beholder as one who is not in the home but out in the street.

NOTES

1   On Metsu's employment of the niche window, a device inspired by Gerrit Dou, see Angela K. Ho, "A Niche of One's Own: Gerrit Dou's Brand-Building Project," in *Creating Distinctions in Dutch Genre Painting: Repetition and Invention* (Amsterdam: Amsterdam University Press, 2017), 53–92; Ronni Baer, "The Paintings of Gerrit Dou (1613–1675)," PhD diss., New York University, 1990; Martha Hollander, *An Entrance for the Eyes: Space & Meaning in Seventeenth-Century Dutch Art* (Berkeley: University of California Press, 2002), 53–57; and Peter Hecht, *De Hollandse fijnschilders: Van Gerard Dou tot Adriaen Van der Werff* (Amsterdam: Rijksmuseum, 1989), 18–19. See also the discussion of the window motif in Mariët Westermann, *The Amusements of Jan Steen: Comic Painting in the Seventeenth Century* (Seattle: University of Washington Press, 1998), 138–42.

2   Horst Wenzel, "Die Verkündigung an Maria. Zur Visualisierung des Wortes in der Szene oder: Schriftgeschichte im Bild," in *Maria in der Welt: Marienverehrung im Kontext der Sozialgeschichte 10.–18. Jahrhundert*, ed. Claudia Opitz, Hedwig Röckelein, Gabriela Signori, and Guy P. Marchal (Zürich: Chronos, 1993), 23–52; Bernhard Siegert, "Vögel, Engel und Gesandte: Alteuropas Übertragungsmedien," in *Gespräche, Boten, Briefe: Körpergedächtnis und Schriftgedächtnis im Mittelalter*, ed. Horst Wenzel (Berlin: E. Schmidt, 1997), 45–62; Christopher P. Heuer, "Die Botschaft als Akteur bei Konrad Witz," in *The Announcement: Annunciations and Beyond*, ed. Hana Gründler, Alessandro Nova, and Itay Sapir (Munich: De Gruyter, 2020), 74–86; and Shira Brisman, "Nachrichten aus Nürnberg: The Annunciation as an Epistolary Address," *Zeitschrift für Kunstgeschichte* 79 (2016): 49–66.

3   For Dutch treatises advising painters on how to dress members of different social classes, see Karel van Mander, *Het Schilder-Boeck* (Haarlem, 1604), vol. 1, *Den grondt der edel vry schilder-const*, chapter 10, 42v; and Samuel van Hoogstraten,

FIG. 3.5. Jan van Eyck, *The Arnolfini Portrait*, 1434, oil on oak panel, 32 ⅜ × 23 ⅝ in. (82.2 × 60 cm). The National Gallery, London, NG186.

Inleyding tot de hooge schoole der schilderkonst: Anders de zichtbaere werelt (Rotterdam, 1678; facsimile edition, Doornspijk: Davaco, 1969), 229. For sumptuary laws regulating the wearing of velvet, see J. van B., *Een onderscheyt boeckje ofte tractaetje vande fouten en dwalingen der politie* (Amsterdam, 1662), 2–4.

4   See, by comparison, the discussion of Rembrandt's painting in Volker Manuth, "Minerva in Her Study" (2017), in *The Leiden Collection Catalogue*, 3rd ed., ed. Arthur K. Wheelock Jr. and Lara Yeager-Crasselt, 2020–, http://www.theleidencollection.com/artwork/minerva-in-her-study/.

5   Adriaan E. Waiboer, "Woman Reading a Book by a Window" in *The Leiden Collection Catalogue*, ed. Arthur K. Wheelock Jr., 2017, http://www.theleidencollection.com/artwork/a-woman-reading-a-letter-by-a-window/. She is called "an allegory for history and antiquity itself—the utterly located Renaissance woman of the male imagining" in Amanda L. Capern, *The Routledge History of Women in Early Modern Europe* (New York: Routledge, 2020), 416.

6   A similar case is made for the use of reds in the "affective fields" of Rembrandt's *Rebecca and Isaac* in Nicola Suthor, *Rembrandt's Roughness* (Princeton, NJ: Princeton University Press, 2018), 172.

7   Their conditions of insecurity are made vivid, for example, in a repository of intercepted letters that left the Dutch Republic but were brought to England when the ships were captured by privateers during the Disaster Year of 1672. Judith Brouwer, *Levenstekens: Gekaapte Brieven uit het Rampjaar 1672* (Hilversum: Verloren, 2014).

8   Peter C. Sutton, "Love Letters: Dutch Genre Paintings in the Age of Vermeer," in *Love Letters: Dutch Genre Paintings in the Age of Vermeer*, ed. Peter C. Sutton et al. (London: Frances Lincoln, 2003), 19–22, cats. 18–19, 131–33; and Ann Jensen Adams, "'Der sprechende Brief.' Kunst des Lesens, Kunst des Schreibens: Schriftkunde un schoonschrijft in den Niederlanden im 17. Jahrhundert," in *Leselust: Niederländische Malerei von Rembrandt bis Vermeer*, ed. Ann Jensen Adams and Sabine Schulze (Frankfurt am Main: Schirn Kunsthalle Frankfurt, 1993), 69–92.

9   Debra Pincus, "Giovanni Bellini's Humanist Signature: Pietro Bembo, Aldus Manutius and Humanism in Early Sixteenth-Century Venice," *Artibus et Historiae* 29, no. 58 (2008): 89–119; Shira Brisman, *Albrecht Dürer and the Epistolary Mode of Address* (Chicago: University of Chicago Press, 2017), 13; and Mariët Westermann, *Art and Home: Dutch Interiors in the Age of Rembrandt* (Zwolle: Waanders, 2001), 90.

10   Mieke Bal, "Reading Bathsheba: From Mastercodes to Misfits," in *Rembrandt's Bathsheba Reading King David's Letter*, ed. Ann Jensen Adams (New York: Cambridge University Press, 1998), 119–20.

11   Bryan J. Wolf, *Vermeer and the Invention of Seeing* (Chicago: University of Chicago Press, 2001), 110 and 84.

12   Bal, "Reading Bathsheba," 119.

13   Ruth Bernard Yeazell, *Picture Titles: How and Why Western Paintings Acquired Their Names* (Princeton, NJ: Princeton University Press, 2015), 28 and 124.

14   John Michael Montias, "How Notaries and Other Scribes Recorded Works of Art in Seventeenth-Century Sales and Inventories," *Simiolus: Netherlands Quarterly for the History of Art* 30, no. 3/4 (2003): 217. For the analysis of 29 notebooks of auction records conducted by Orphan Chamber of Amsterdam, dating from 1597 to 1638, see John Michael Montias, *Art at Auction in 17th Century Amsterdam* (Amsterdam: Amsterdam University Press, 2002). For information from 1,280 Amsterdam inventories of goods dating from 1597 to 1681 and drawing from the *Gemeentearchief* (now known as the *Stadsarchief*), see the Montias Database: http://research.frick.org/montias.

15   Julie Hardwick, *The Practice of Patriarchy: Gender and the Politics of Household Authority in Early Modern France* (University Park: Pennsylvania State University Press, 1998), 20. For more on the history of the profession and its representation in art, see E. M. Marck and Marianne Eisma, *De Notaris in Woord en Beeld: De Cultuurhistorische Collectie van de Stichting tot Bevordering der Notariële Wetenschap* (Zwolle: Waanders, 2013).

16   M. T. Clancy, *From Memory to Written Record: England 1066–1307*, 2nd ed. (Oxford: Blackwell, 1993), 305; and Kathryn Burns, "Notaries, Truth, and Consequences," *The American Historical Review* 110, no. 2 (2005): 372.

17   Ilja M. Veldman, *De Wereld tussen goed en kwaad: Late prenten van Coornhert* (The Hague: SDU, 1990), 23–26; Huigen Leeflang, *Hendrick Goltzius: New Hollstein Dutch and Flemish Etchings, Engravings, and Woodcuts, 1450–1700*, vol. 1 (Ouderkerk aan den IJssel: Sound and Vision Publishers, 2012), xlv; Alain Wijffels, "Lawyers and Litigants: The Corrupting Appeal and Effects of Civil Litigation in Hendrick Goltzius' Litis abusus," *The Art of Law: Artistic Representations and Iconography of Law and Justice in Context*, ed. Stefan Huygebaert et al. (Cham: Springer, 2018), 181–96; and Henk Bonger and Gerrit Voogt, *The Life and Work of Dirck Volkertszoon Coornhert* (Amsterdam: Rodopi, 2004), 28–35.

18   Notary Public, H. Westfrisius, Gemeentearchief Amsterdam, notarieel archief no. 2801, fol. 307, 19-7-1657; Abraham Bredius, "Iets over de jeugd van Gabriël Metsu," *Oud Holland* 25 (1907): 197–203; and Linda Stone-Ferrier, "Gabriel Metsu's Vegetable Market at Amsterdam: Seventeenth-Century Dutch Market Paintings and Horticulture," *Art Bulletin* 71, no. 3 (1989): 448.

19   Gemeentearchief Amsterdam, notarieel archief no. 2977, fols. 639-40; and Adriaan E. Waiboer, "The Early Years of Gabriel Metsu," *Burlington Magazine* 147, no. 1223 (2005): 90, fn. 59.

20   Gemeentearchief Leiden, notarieel archief no. 621, fol. 106; Bredius, "Iets over de jeugd," 198.

21   Walter S. Melion, "Memory and the Kinship of Writing and Picturing in the Early Seventeenth-Century Netherlands," *Word and Image* 8 (1992): 48–70; Croiset van Uchelen, *Nederlandse schrijfmeesters uit de zeventiende eeuw* (The Hague: Rijksmuseum Meermanno-Westreenianum, 1978), 17–20; David P. Becker, *The Practice of Letters: The Hofer Collection of Writing Manuals 1514–1800* (Cambridge, MA: Harvard College Library, 1997), no. 100, 54–55; Ann Jensen Adams, "Disciplining the Hand, Disciplining the Heart: Letter-Writing Paintings and Practices in Seventeenth-Century Holland," in *Love Letters*, 69; and H. A. Warmelink, *De Notarissen, de calligraphie en de drukkunst, De Bibliographie van het notariaat* (Wageningen: Gebr. Zomer en Keuning, 1952).

22   Jan van den Velde, *Spieghel der schrijfkonste* (Amsterdam: Willem Blaeu, 1608), n.p. [72v]; and Melion, "Memory and the Kinship of Writing and Picturing," 58.

23   Adriaan Pitlo, *De zeventiende en achttiende eeuwse Notarisboeken: een verhandeling over notarisboeken, notarisambt en notarieel recht onder de republiek der Verenigde Nederlanden* (Amsterdam: Stichting tot Bevordering der Notariële Wetenschap, [1948] 2004), 132–34.

24   For a discussion of the gestures of concealment in Metsu's painting of the notary, whereby the "openbaer Notarus" is understood ironically because the notary does not reveal the inside of his office or the nature of his notarial document, see Maarten L. Wurfbain, "Vrouwenfiguren in schilderijen uit Gabriël Metsu's Leidse jaren," *Tableau* 2, no. 1 (October/November 1979), 14–18.

25   The last digit is no longer legible, and may have initially read "1653," but my assessment, based on the style and content of the work, is that it more likely read "1655." For a discussion of the date on this and other Metsu paintings, see Adriaan E. Waiboer, *Gabriel Metsu, Life and Work: A Catalogue Raisonné* (New Haven, CT: Yale University Press, 2012), 161.

26   Melion, "Memory and the Kinship of Writing and Picturing," 50n20.

27   Van Mander, *Het Schilder-Boeck*, vol. 1, fol. 51v.

28   Erwin Panofsky, "Jan van Eyck's Arnolfini Portrait," *Burlington Magazine for Connoisseurs* 64, no. 372 (1934): 124. For more on Van Eyck acting as a notary, see the commentary on his signature, "Actu[m] an[n]o domini 1432 10 die octobris a ioh[anne] de Eck" (Completed on 10 October 1432 by Jan van Eyck) on the painting of Tymotheos. The word *actum* was used at the closure of a notarial deed to introduce the place, date, and witness. Jacques Paviot, "The Sitter for Jan van Eyck's 'Leal Sovvenir,'" *Journal of the Warburg and Courtauld Institutes* 58 (1995): 212; and Wendy Wood, "A New Identification of the Sitter in Jan van Eyck's Tymotheos Portrait," *Art Bulletin* 60, no. 4 (1978): 653.

29   Margaret L. Koster, "The Arnolfini Double Portrait: A Simple Solution," *Apollo* 158 (September 2003): 3–14.

30   For a more forceful iteration of this statement, "The picture, not Van Eyck the artist, is the witness," see Jonathan Bordo, "Picture and Witness at the Site of the Wilderness," *Critical Inquiry* 26, no. 2 (2000): 234. For more on the "inquiry into the status of images as documents in their own right, not merely as expressions of their artist's prominence," see Linda Seidel, "'Jan van Eyck's Arnolfini Portrait': Business as Usual?," *Critical Inquiry* 16, no. 1 (1989): 59. Seidel also discusses the comparative role of notaries in Van Eyck's Flanders and Arnolfini's native Tuscany, 68.

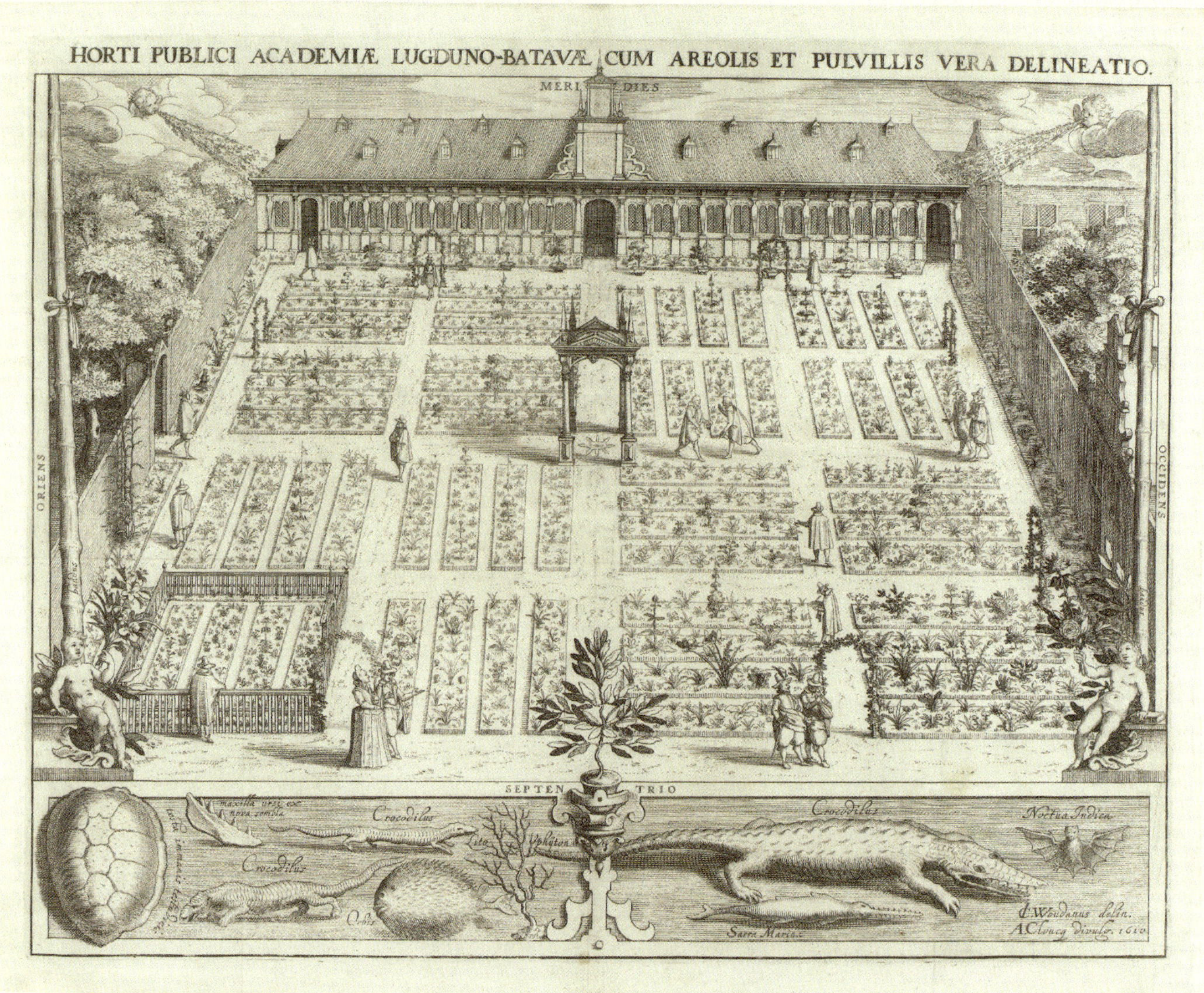

HORTI PUBLICI ACADEMIAE LUGDUNO-BATAVAE CUM AREOLIS ET PULVILLIS VERA DELINEATIO.
MERIDIES
ORIENS
OCCIDENS
SEPTENTRIO
Crocodilus
Crocodilus
Crocodilus
Noctua Indica
Orbis
Sara Maris
E. Woudanus delin.
A. Clouc divulg. 1610

An Eye for Detail:
Art, Science, and Religion in
Seventeenth-Century Leiden

Eric Jorink

Fascination with detail was pervasive in seventeenth-century Leiden. Among other things, the city's fame was based on the manufacture of cloth, the production of cutting-edge scholarship, and the work of the Leiden *fijnschilders* (fine painters). What the three had in common was an eye for texture, structure, and minute detail. Textiles, texts, and paintings were all products of ingenuity and skill, as well as of entrepreneurship, contributing to the luster and wealth of the city. The paintings of the *fijnschilders* exemplify this world of businessmen, scholars, and burghers. These works of art invoke a sense of intimacy between the women and men portrayed, the objects they hold, and the quiet, solemn spaces in which they are caught in the act of studying them. The *fijnschilders'* sitters observe and handle books, manuscripts, flowers, antiquities, works of art, scientific instruments, and an occasional skull with a sincere hand and a faithful eye (see FIG. 2.4). The sober settings of their portraits invite contemplation and introspection, while the meticulous representation of the objects within these spaces betrays a captivation by the visible world. At the same time, these detailed domestic scenes can suggest a higher truth, evoking the spiritual in the everyday. Caught in the act of contemplating a book or an object, the men and women portrayed here invite the viewer, in turn, to share in their thoughts.

In this chapter, we will examine links between Leiden's emergence as a center for paintings of "an inner world" and the role of Leiden University, the first and by far the most important center of learning in the Netherlands. As we will see, the worlds of art and the sciences *(de wetenschappen)* overlapped.[1] Cultivating an eye for detail through reading, studying, observing, representing, and contemplating was as key to the scholar's work as it was to the *fijnschilder's*, and many Leiden artists had links with the university. Likewise, some Leiden professors took great delight in the work of the city's most notable *fijnschilders*, moved by their shared enchantment with things minute and intricate.

READING THE BOOK OF NATURE

Established in 1575, Leiden's was the first university in the Northern Netherlands[2] and trained generations of both Dutch and international students in law, medicine, and theology. Housed in confiscated Catholic buildings, it became the Dutch Republic's center for Protestant learning. It also had a strong impact on civic and cultural life in the city of Leiden. Within two

Jan Cornelisz van 't Woudt, engraved by Willem Isaacsz van Swanenburg, *Hortus Botanicus van de Universiteit Leiden*, 1610, etching and engraving, 12 ⅞ × 15 ⅞ in. (32.8 × 40.4 cm). Rijksmuseum, Amsterdam, RP-P-1893-A-18089.

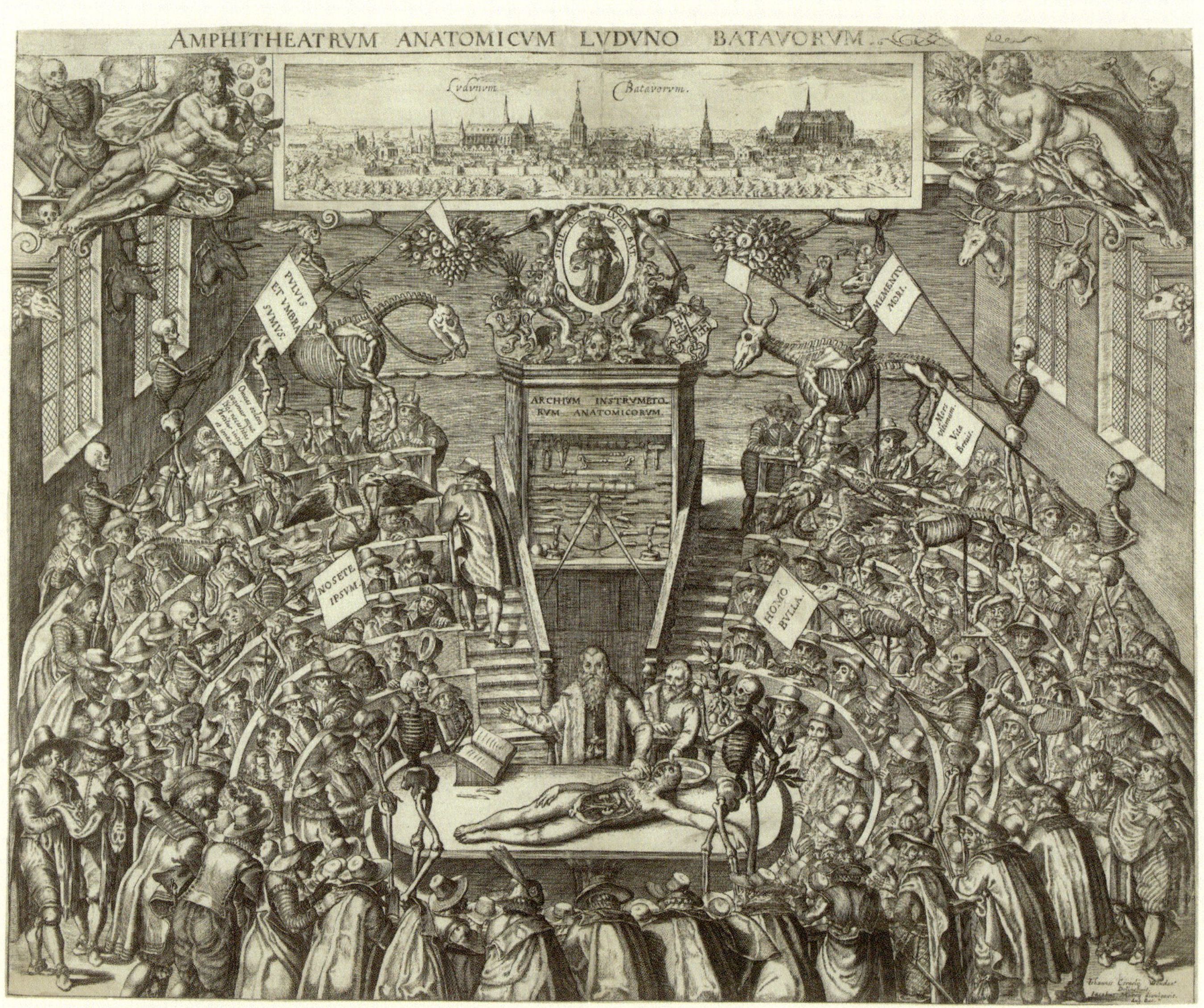
AMPHITHEATRVM ANATOMICVM LVDVNO BATAVORVM
Ludunm.
Batavorum.
PVLVIS ET VMBRA SVMVS
MEMENTO MORI
NOSCE TE IPSVM
HOMO BVLLA
MERI VITA brevis.
ARCHIVM INSTRVMETO- RVM ANATOMICORVM.

decades, Leiden University was one of the most flourishing universities in Europe, not least due to its botanical garden and anatomical theater (FIGS. 4.1 and 4.2).[3] These two institutions supported the teaching in the faculty of medicine, but they were also open to the general public. Until the sixteenth century, the world of learning had focused on reading books (mostly the Bible and the classics) to glean the knowledge they contained. As the century progressed, due to the advance of humanism in Northern Italy, science and education became more visual and tactile—including dissections, the cultivation of botanical gardens, and hands-on sessions with coins, antiquities, works of art, and all kind of "rarities"—embracing a new spirit of discovery. Library (*bibliotheca*) was more or less synonymous with *studiolo, scrittoio, galleria*, cabinet, *musaeum*, and *orbis in domo*: a place for study and contemplation—no longer of books only, but also of specimens and treasures. It was a solemn room for solitude and scholarship, for reflecting on the world.[4] Not only did scholars and princes surround themselves with precious objects; so, too, did merchants, regents (civic and social leaders), and *liefhebbers* (enthusiasts).[5] In the Protestant north of Europe, much emphasis was put on the study of the Bible as well—including the study of Greek and Hebrew, to promote the interpretation of Scripture in its original languages. Scholars were trained to read, understand, compare, and think about the Word of God carefully; laymen were encouraged to do the same. The level of literacy was high in the Dutch Republic, as becomes evident from the paintings of Leiden's citizens—male and female—who were often depicted in the act of reading (FIG 4.3).

Reading, observing, and looking had strong religious connotations—God had bestowed men with a pair of eyes. According to the Dutch Reformed Church, the Lord revealed himself to humankind via two means: first, of course, was Scripture, which all Christians had to read for themselves; but God, Protestants insisted, also manifested himself through his creation. Did not everything in nature, from the most distant planet to the tiniest blade of grass, betray God's creative power? Echoing Saint Augustine, the articles of faith of the Dutch Reformed Church stated that God made himself known by the Bible and by the Book of Nature.[6]

> We know him [God] by two means. First, by the creation, preservation, and government of the universe, since that universe is before our eyes like a beautiful book in which all creatures, great and small, are as letters *to make us ponder the invisible things of God his eternal power and his divinity*, as the apostle Paul says in Romans 1:20. . . . Second, he makes himself known to us more openly by his holy and divine word.[7]

Nature could be seen and read and, like the Bible, was a revelation by the divine author. All creatures, great and small, were as letters, referring to God. This was a strong encouragement to observe, study, and represent nature, including the smallest of creatures. *Ex minimus patet ipse Deus* ("God shows himself also in the smallest of things") became a common phrase among scholars and artists alike. It was in this context that Protestant artists such as Joris Hoefnagel (1542–1600) and Jacques de Gheyn II (1565–1629) started to show an interest in insects— before that time a rather neglected subject.[8] Did not a faithful representation of their intricate anatomy reveal the power of the creator? At the same time, the new genre of still-life painting emerged, with careful compositions of flowers, insects, and shells some- times suggestively placed in niches where now- detested sculptures of saints were once displayed. Natural objects had a religious meaning, not only

FIG. 4.2. Jan Cornelisz van 't Woudt, engraved by Bartholomeus Willemsz Dolendo, *Theatrum anatomicum van Leidse Academie*, 1609, engraving, 18 ⅛ × 21 ¾ in. (46 × 55.3 cm). Rijksmuseum, Amsterdam, RP-P-1887-A-12041.

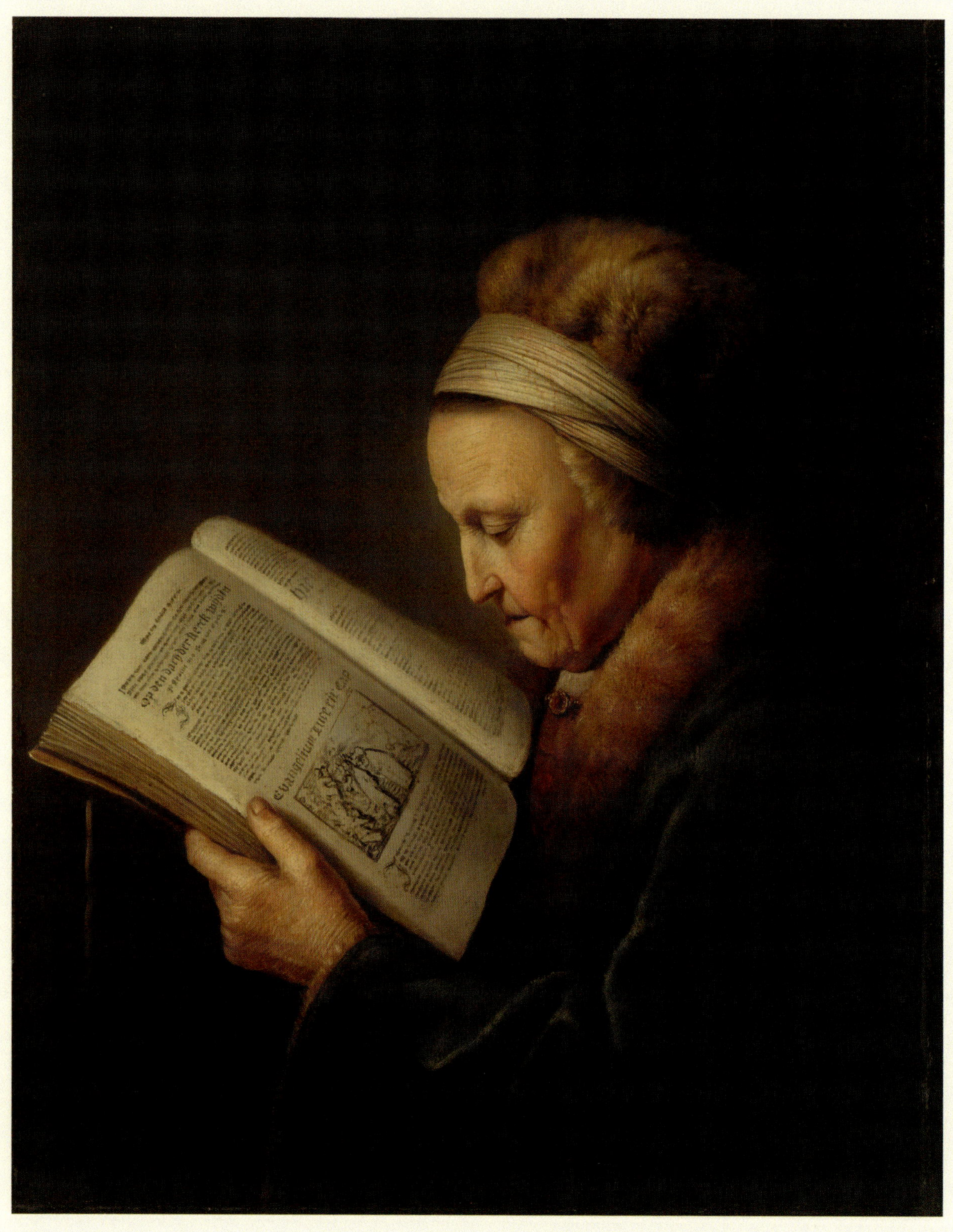

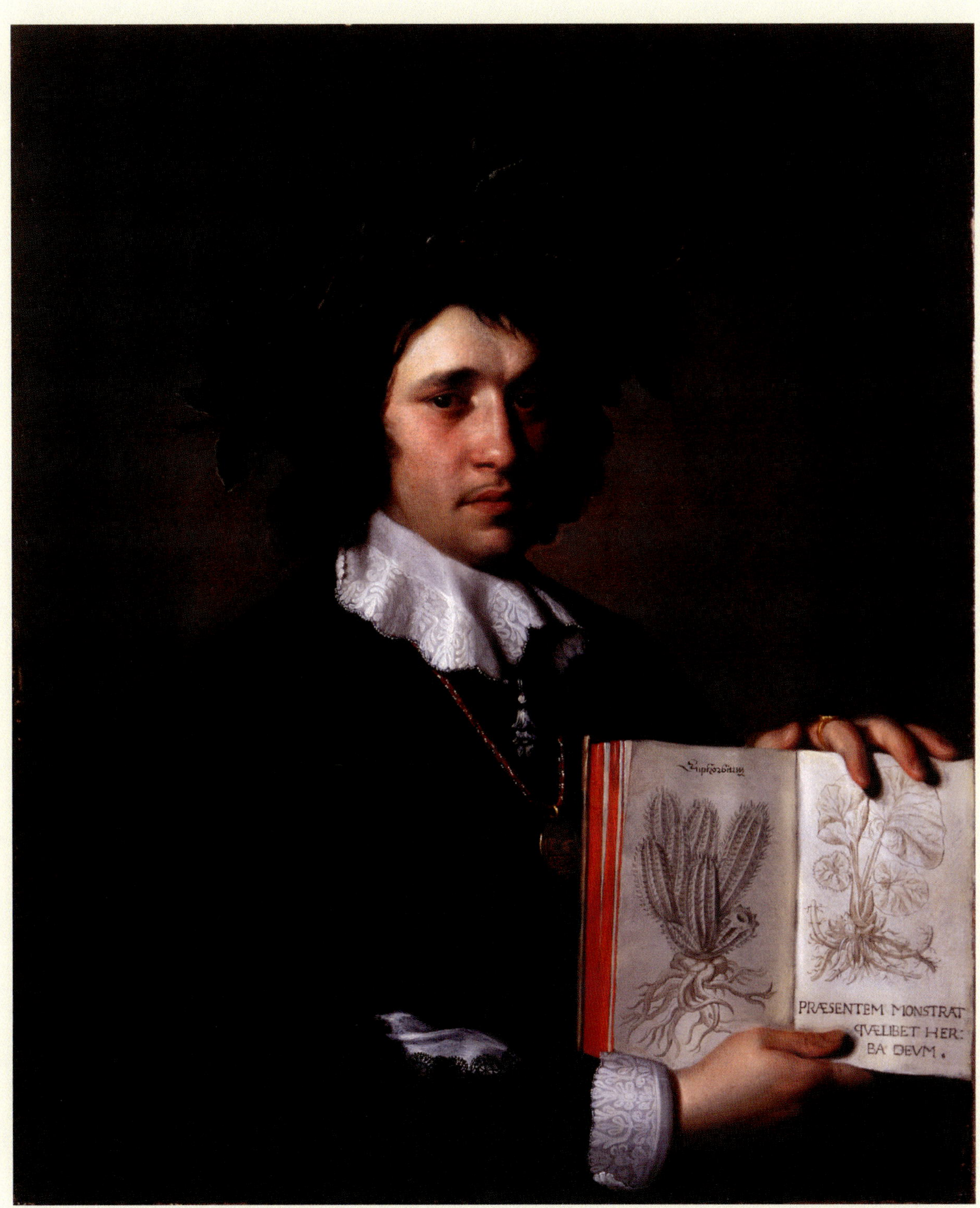

Euphorbium
PRÆSENTEM MONSTRAT
QVÆLIBET HER:
BA DEVM.

because of their biblical and symbolic references, but also because their elaborate structure could only have been created by God. A butterfly could be seen both as a reference to the resurrection of the dead and as a product of God's marvelous design. The notion that the tiniest sprig could refer to the power of the Lord finds expression in a portrait by Willem Moreelse (1618/23–1666) that depicts a newly minted doctoral graduate holding a botanical book inscribed, "Every herb shows the presence of God" (FIG 4.4).

All Leiden professors had to subscribe to the Dutch Reformed articles of faith, including the doctrine of the Book of Nature. Indeed, reading and studying nature was at the core of the university's educational program. Leiden scholars also excelled in the study of the Bible—clarifying and comparing translations with original texts, parsing problematic and sometimes contradictory lines. Joseph Justus Scaliger (1540–1609), by far the most famous humanist of his age, trained a generation of biblical scholars, including Hugo Grotius (1583–1645). In the almost-sacred silence of their *musaea*, humanists studied the Hebrew and Greek texts of the Old and New Testaments in philological detail. Many Dutch citizens did the same—sometimes in the vernacular, sometimes in the ancient tongues. Nearly every household held at least one Bible; reading and contemplating Scripture was akin to having a private conversation with God. Sitting alone, studying the Word of God by candlelight was an act of devotion. Paintings of the devout reading the Bible in absolute solitude sometimes evoke similar scenes of hermits, such as *Hermit Praying in the Wilderness* (cat. 6) by Willem van Mieris (1662–1747). Scaliger was portrayed in a red gown reminiscent of

the iconography of Saint Jerome (FIG. 4.5), the prolific biblical scholar whose Latin translation of the Bible is known as the Vulgate.

Leiden University provided opportunities for its students as well as the public to learn from God's "second revelation" in nature. Its botanical garden and anatomical theater opened in 1595. These were new means of education, intended for the instruction of medical students through visual and material objects, but as noted above, both were also open to the public—including women. At the botanical garden, visitors could see plants described by the ancients and new flora brought back from the East Indies. Moreover, in the gallery, a natural history collection—with specimens including crocodiles, blowfish, and corals—was displayed in close connection to books and maps, such as Pliny's *Natural History* and the works of the botanical garden's director, Carolus Clusius. In the anatomical theater, a human corpse (the body of an executed criminal) was publicly dissected once a year.[9] This was a celebrated public event, presenting lessons on the delicate anatomy of the human body as well as on the transience of life. Young Rembrandt van Rijn (1606–1669), a student of Leiden University between 1620 and 1622, witnessed one of the dissections performed there.[10] Organized by the medical faculty, the autopsies supported the students' education and excited the senses. Conducted by candlelight, anatomical dissections also had a strongly religious character, vividly illustrating the doctrines of life and death, sin and punishment, as well as the ingenuity of the human fabric.[11] The events' moral lessons were reinforced by the skeletons adorning the theater, some carrying banners with humanist mottoes

FIG. 4.3. Gerrit Dou, *Old Woman Reading*, ca. 1631–32, oil on panel, 28 × 21 ¾ in. (71.2 × 55.2 cm). Rijksmuseum, Amsterdam: A. H. Hoekwater Bequest, The Hague, SK-A-2627.

FIG. 4.4. Willem Moreelse, *Portrait of a Scholar*, 1647, oil on canvas, 32 ⅝ × 26 ⅜ in. (82.8 × 67 cm). Toledo Museum of Art: Purchased with funds from the Libbey Endowment, Gift of Edward Drummond Libbey, 1962.70.

Willem van Mieris, *Hermit Praying in the Wilderness*, 1707, oil on panel, 8 ¼ × 6 ⅞ in. (21 × 17.4 cm). The Leiden Collection, New York.

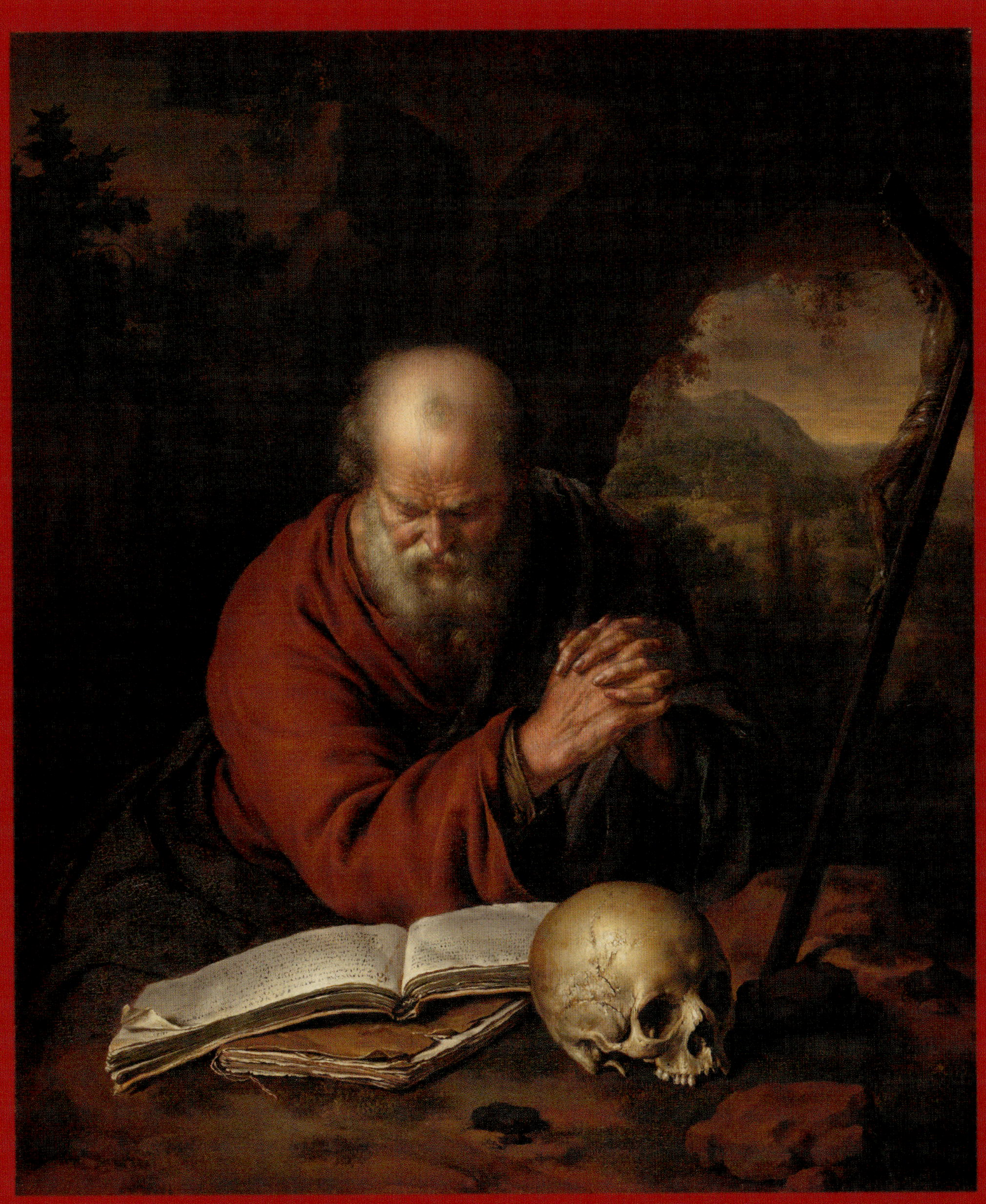

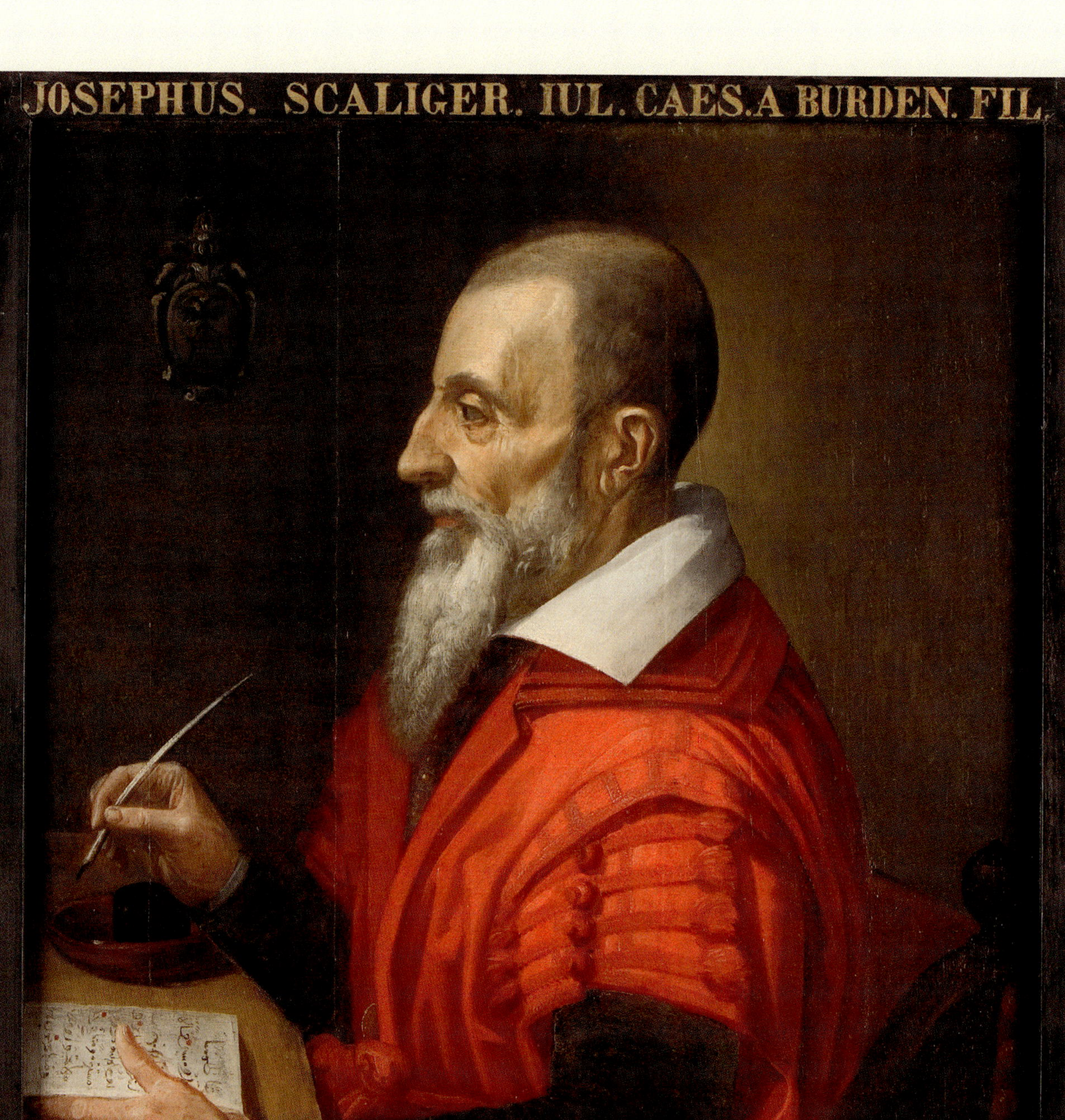

JOSEPHUS. SCALIGER. IUL. CAES. A BURDEN. FIL.
ACADEMIAE LUGD.-BAT. DECUS INDE A.
D. 28 AUGUSTI. A. 1593. NATUS AQUINNI
NITIOBRIGUM. NONIS AUGUSTI. A. 1540.
OBIIT D. 21 IANUAR. A. 1609.

like *Homo bulla* ("man is nothing but a bubble"). In a vignette alluding to the act of original sin and the resulting expulsion from Paradise, two skeletons representing Adam and Eve posed beside the Tree of Knowledge. As in the botanical garden, a collection featuring all kinds of rarities was on display at the anatomical theater, ranging from Egyptian mummies to stuffed anteaters. To record those sites of knowledge for posterity, De Gheyn and Woudanus engraved detailed images of both garden and theater (see FIGS. 4.1 and 4.2).[12]

LOOKING AT SMALL THINGS

Following the example of the Leiden University collections, many citizens started collections of rarities of their own. Precious stones, dried herbs, shells, and a variety of insects all testified that even the smallest characters in the Book of Nature were created by God. Their diminutive size and intricate structure were understood to reflect His divine wisdom and power. Insects, especially, became a source of wonder. In the wake of Hoefnagel, and with the aid of the newly invented microscope after 1620, scientists wondered at the previously unseen and unknown structures of the smallest of creatures. Bees, butterflies, and ants had already been depicted in the Middle Ages, but now hundreds if not thousands of other species became *en vogue*. Around 1625, Jacques de Gheyn toyed with the idea of making a series of drawings of the "New World" seen under the microscope. Some decades later, Johannes Swammerdam (1637–1680), a Leiden medical student, was one of the first in Europe to study insects systematically (FIG. 4.6). Referring to the doctrine of the Book of Nature, he wrote in the *Historia naturalis insectorum* (1669) and later works that in studying much-despised creatures like lice, beetles, and dragonflies, one had to be as attentive and precise, as faithful and accurate as in studying the verses of the

Bible. Being a skilled artist as well, he took great care to depict the results of his dissections in the most accurate way. Fanciful and clumsy representations were no less than blasphemous. And, like reflecting on the Bible, contemplating God's creatures could also be a very a private affair.

The introduction of the microscope encouraged other fields of inquiry as well. Texture and structure became a new focus of attention. Swammerdam had already drawn a comparison between the fabric of textiles and the tissue of humans and animals, but Leiden scholars sought to learn just what composed the fabric of the human body. What, they wondered, constitutes matter, structure, and color? Does nature consist of tiny, nearly invisible particles, as the great philosopher René Descartes (1596–1650)—who lived and published in Leiden—claimed? Are those intricate building blocks of matter and life visible under the microscope? Is it possible to transfer one matter into another, as alchemists since ancient times had believed? And how could the visible world be represented in texts and images, from scholarly treatises to edifying artworks?

FRANCISCUS DE LA BOË SYLVIUS

The interrogation of the physical world triggered a philosophical ripple effect among scholars and artisans, as exemplified by Franciscus de la Boë Sylvius (1614–1672), professor of medicine at Leiden University from 1658 until his death. Studying the human fabric and physiology in microscopic detail, he elaborated on the idea of the body as a divine piece of engineering, as a great work of art. Sylvius educated a generation of physicians who went on to staff medical faculties and courts all over Europe. To historians of art, he is mostly known for his patronage of Frans van Mieris the Elder.[13] Sylvius had studied in Leiden, where he, of course, took lessons in the botanical garden and anatomical

FIG. 4.5. Attributed to Jan Cornelisz van 't Woudt, *Portrait of Joseph Justus Scaliger (1540–1609)*, ca. 1608, oil on panel, 27 ⁹⁄₁₆ × 24 in. (70 × 61 cm). Leiden University, Icones Leidenses 31.

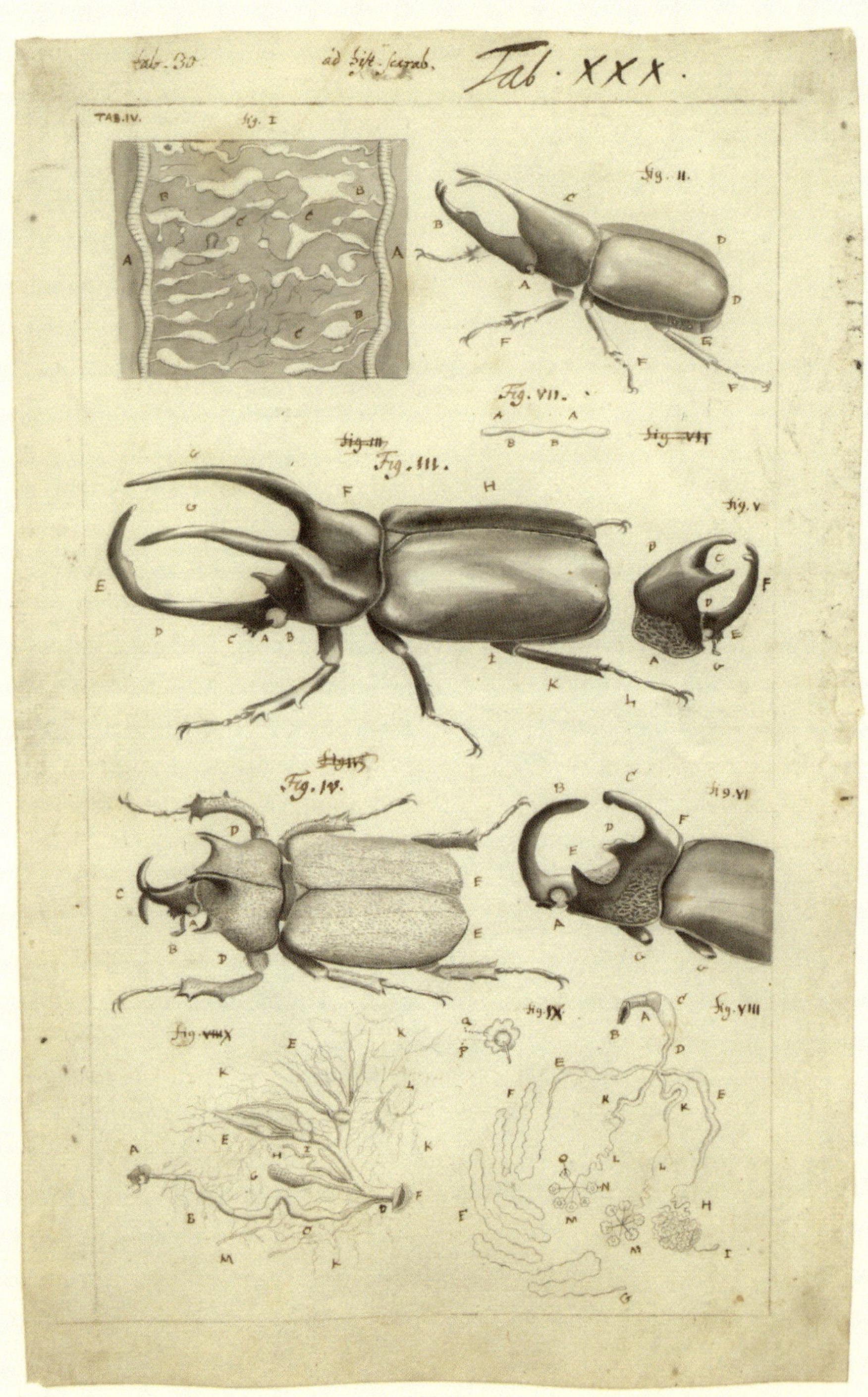
TAB. IV.
Fig. I
Fig. II.
Fig. VII.
Fig. III.
Fig. V.
Fig. IV.
Fig. VI.
Fig. VIII
Fig. IX

theater. In 1637, he received his medical doctorate. Sylvius was much inspired by the new philosophy of Descartes, as well as by alchemical theories. Both believed that the world consisted of minute particles, tiny *corpuscula* interfering with one another. After his study, Sylvius settled into a practice in Amsterdam, where he continued his interest in chemistry and alchemy. The disciplines were closely related. Contrary to what is often believed, alchemy was a respected branch of science, with strongly religious undertones, as many of its practitioners posited that the transmutation of base metals into gold was a metaphor for the imperfect human soul striving toward God.[14] The more practical, experimental, and hands-on study of metals and other elements revealed something of the deeper, inner structure and subtility of God's grand design. For decades, Sylvius ran alchemical experiments, exploring the boundaries of matter and spirit, of science and art. Bodily engagement with metals and acids instructed his views not only on the human fabric, but also on the new and noble art of etching. Besides having a lucrative medical practice and conducting experiments, Sylvius garnered a fortune by discovering *sal volatile* (a form of smelling salts), one of the results of his chemical interests. After being appointed as professor of medicine in Leiden in 1658, he built a monumental (and still extant) house just one hundred meters from the university on the Rapenburg canal, the preferred neighborhood of regents, wealthy merchants, and university professors.

In his teaching and research, Sylvius focused on the inner structure of the human body, including the barely visible glands, nerves, and tissues. Once again, an eye for detail was key here. Without comprehending the more subtle structure of bodies, one could not understand the whole—and vice versa. Considering the body as a laboratory, Sylvius studied the circulation of fluids in great detail, often with the aid of the microscope.

His many students did the same; they all were fascinated by the fabric of human and animal bodies. In the anatomical theater, but also at Sylvius's home, he and his students dissected dogs, frogs, and other small creatures, as well as, incidentally, a human corpse. The professor and four of his most famous students—Swammerdam along with Nicolas Steno (1638–1686), Frederik Ruysch (1638–1731), and Regnier de Graaf (1641–1673)—had a great interest in the visual arts, and all were exceptionally good at drawing. Discovering and representing microstructures was their main interest. In the same spirit, Sylvius continued his alchemical research: his house included no fewer than three rooms with furnaces where he could experiment with metals, acids, bases, and all kinds of other organic and inorganic materials. Here, tiny particles and minute details were the focus of attention as well. Not only was it a respectable yet mysterious field of inquiry, but it promised to open a way to divine knowledge. At the same time Sylvius was experimenting in Leiden, young Isaac Newton (1643–1727) developed similar interests in Cambridge. We see the same sympathetic perception reflected in Jacob Toorenvliet's (1640–1719) *Alchemist* from 1684 (cat. 10). More than twenty years earlier, Ole Borch (1626–1690), a Danish colleague of Sylvius's who was similarly fascinated by alchemy, had visited Toorenvliet in his workshop, where he also recorded seeing "exceptionally fine work" by Gerrit Dou (1613–1675).[15]

Sylvius was interested not only in anatomy and alchemy, but also in the arts and sciences in a far broader sense. The inventory of his house has survived, and from that we learn about the presence of the furnaces and a room for dissecting, as well as a library, rarities and instruments, a workshop for carving ivory and wood, and a splendid collection of art.[16] Besides many engravings and etchings, Sylvius owned roughly 180 paintings, one of the

FIG. 4.6. Johannes Swammerdam, study of staghorn beetle and other beetles, both life size and under the microscope, table XXX from *Icones operis Biblia naturae*, 1675, manuscript, 15 3/16 × 9 13/16 in. (38.5 × 25 cm). Leiden University Libraries Special Collections.

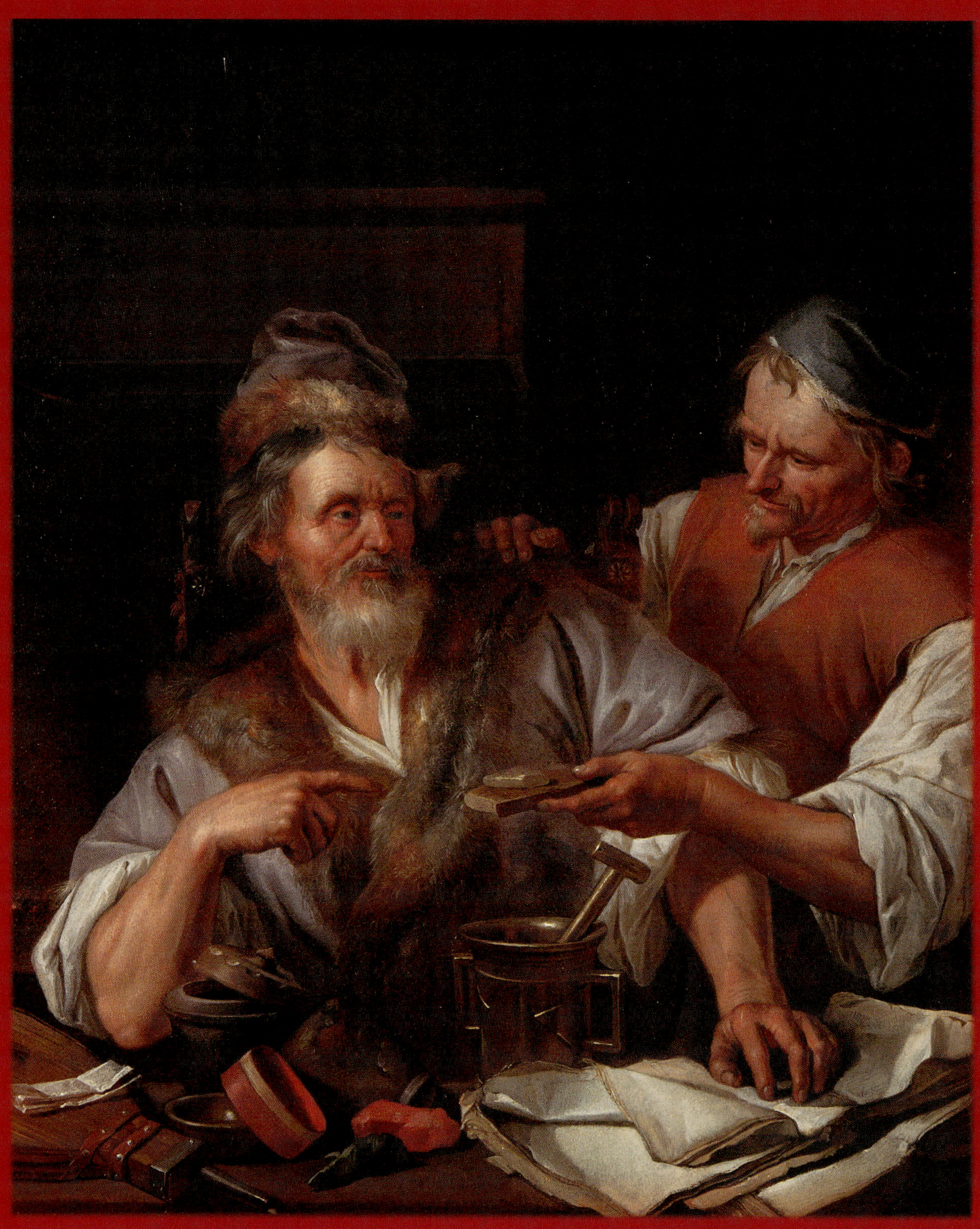

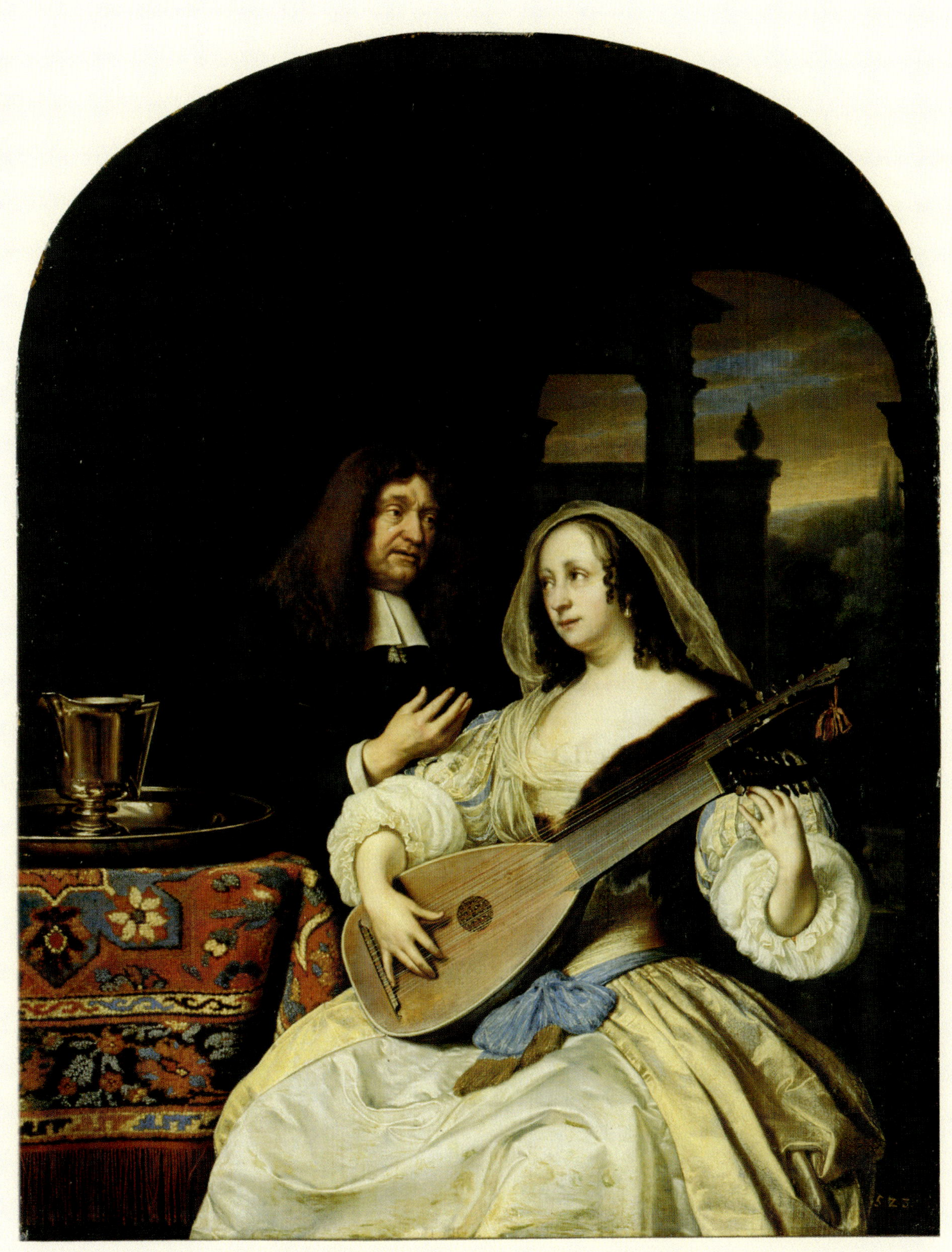

largest collections in town. He had little interest in historical, mythological, and religious paintings in the narrative, Italian style. Nor was he much interested in Dutch genre paintings in the style of Jan Steen (1626–1679). His taste ran to "the art of describing" (to borrow a term from art historian Svetlana Alpers), to artists who painted meticulous naturalistic renderings of objects, animals, and humans.[17] Besides owning works by Roelant Savery (1576–1639) and Paulus Potter (1625–1654), Sylvius took great delight in the Leiden *fijnschilders*, particularly Van Mieris. The professor often visited the painter in his workshop, gave Van Mieris commissions, and had the first right to purchase his latest works. It was Sylvius who introduced Van Mieris to Cosimo de' Medici during the latter's visit to the Dutch Republic in 1668. Subsequently, the future archduke ordered some works by "Miris, pittore assai celebre" (Van Mieris, the very famous painter).[18] In 1672, after Sylvius's wife had died, the widower had Van Mieris paint a memorial portrait (FIG. 4.7). The delicate structure and shine of his late wife's silk robe immediately catch the eye. At his death, Sylvius owned seven paintings by Van Mieris and eleven by Gerrit Dou, the most expensive of the Leiden *fijnschilders*. From the inventory, we learn that the paintings, as well as the other works of art and science, were spread throughout the many chambers in the house. Upon entering, visitors and privately tutored students immediately stood face to face with works of art (including *The Quacksalver* by Adrian Brouwer [1605–1638]). Sylvius had 34 paintings in the majestic large salon, 26 in the side chamber, 22 in the dining room, and 42 in the master bedroom, which also housed an impressive number of rarities such as porcelain, shells, lacquered boxes, ivory objects, and two books of prints. It is worth noting that Sylvius also had a large quantity of table linen—at a time when this was still a rarity in other countries, even at noble courts.

Can we discern a connection between the Leiden artists' obsession with detail and Sylvius's fascination with the minute structure of all things? Are not both works of art and the practice of scientific inquiry the result of a shared preoccupation with texture, structure, and sensory perception? All the protagonists in the paintings Sylvius collected are engaged in looking, touching, hearing, tasting, and smelling. It is certainly unsurprising that he, the empirical scientist, owned a series of the Five Senses by Jan Miense Molenaer (1610–1668). As Pamela H. Smith put it, an examination of Sylvius's house and art collection gives us insight "into the cultural and epistemological concerns common both to the new philosophy and to aesthetics in the seventeenth century. . . . Both Sylvius's new philosophy and his collection of 'new' paintings are expressions of a new view of the world and a new approach to nature, part of a profound shift in the orientation of European culture toward material things."[19]

With the description of Sylvius's house, and through the reconstruction of his collection of paintings by the Leiden *fijnschilders* and other works of art, exotic objects, chemical utensils, and scientific instruments, we catch a glimpse of the "inner world" of seventeenth-century Leiden. It was a sanctum where words and things, body and soul, matter and metaphysics overlapped. It was a microcosm, a safe space to contemplate all letters, large and small, of the great book of the world.

Jacob Toorenvliet, *Alchemist*, 1684, oil on copper, 12 7/16 × 10 in. (31.6 × 25.3 cm). The Leiden Collection, New York.

FIG. 4.7. Frans van Mieris the Elder, *Portrait of Franciscus de la Boë Sylvius and His Wife*, 1672, oil on oak panel, 16 1/8 × 16 7/8 in. (41 × 43 cm). Gemäldegalerie Alte Meister, Dresden, Gal.-Nr. 1743.

NOTES

1   For the Dutch context of this topic, see Eric Jorink and Bart Ramakers, eds., *Art and Science in the Early Modern Low Countries*, Netherlands Yearbook for History of Art / Nederlands Kunsthistorisch Jaarboek 62 (Zwolle: WBooks, 2012).

2   Theodoor Herman Lunsingh Scheurleer and G. H. M. Posthumus Meyjes, eds., *Leiden University in the Seventeenth Century: An Exchange of Learning* (Leiden: Leiden University Press, 1975); and Willem Otterspeer, *Het bolwerk van de vrijheid: De Leidse universiteit, 1575–1672* (Amsterdam: Bert Bakker, 2000).

3   Tim Huisman, *The Finger of God: Anatomical Practice in 17th-Century Leiden* (Leiden: Primavera, 2009).

4   Paula Findlen, "The Museum: Its Classical Etymology and Renaissance Genealogy," *Journal of the History of Collections* 1 (1989): 59–78; Ellinoor Bergvelt and Reneé Kistemaker, eds., *De wereld binnen handbereik: Nederlandse kunst- en rariteitenverzamelingen, 1585–1735*, 2 vols. (Zwolle: Amsterdams Historisch Museum, 1992); and Arthur MacGregor, *Curiosity and Enlightenment: Collectors and Collections from the Sixteenth to the Nineteenth Century* (New Haven, CT: Yale University Press, 2010).

5   Lara Yeager-Crasselt, "Knowledge and Practice Pictured in the Artist's Studio: The 'Art Lover' in the Seventeenth-Century Netherlands," *De Zeventiende Eeuw* 32, no. 2 (2016): 185–210; and Eric Jorink, Anne-Sophie Lehmann, and Bart Ramakers, eds., *Lessons in Art: Art, Education and Modes of Instruction since 1500*, Netherlands Yearbook for History of Art / Nederlands Kunsthistorisch Jaarboek 68 (Leiden: Brill, 2019).

6   Eric Jorink, *Reading the Book of Nature in the Dutch Golden Age, 1575–1715* (Leiden: Brill, 2010).

7   Jan Nicolaas Bakhuizen van den Brink, *De Nederlandse belijdenisgeschriften*, 2nd ed. (Amsterdam: Bolland, 1976), 73.

8   Eric Jorink, "Insects, Philosophy and the Microscope," in *Worlds of Natural History*, ed. Helen Anne Curry, Nicholas Jardine, James Andrew Secord, and Emma C. Spary (Cambridge: Cambridge University Press, 2018), 131–50; Marisa Bass, *Insect Artifice: Nature and Art in the Dutch Revolt* (Princeton, NJ: Princeton University Press, 2019); Janice Neri, *The Insect and the Image: Visualizing Nature in Early Modern Europe, 1500–1700* (Minneapolis: University of Minnesota Press, 2011); and Claudia Swan, "Illustrated Natural History," in *Prints and the Pursuit of Knowledge in Early Modern Europe*, ed. Susan Dackerman (Cambridge, MA.: Harvard Art Museums, 2011).

9   Huisman, *Finger of God*.

10   J. Schaeps and M. van Duijn, *Rembrandt en de universiteit van Leiden* (Leiden: Leiden University Press, 2019). Rembrandt, whose earliest paintings are a series on the five senses, remained fascinated with the sensory throughout his long career.

11   In the face of earlier Catholic opposition to human dissection, Dutch Protestants were careful to justify such spectacles from a religious point of view. On the religious connotations of anatomical instruction, see Huisman, *Finger of God*, and Jorink, *Reading the Book of Nature*.

12   De Gheyn made engravings of the botanical garden in 1601 and the anatomical theater in 1609; Swanenburg engraved drawings after Woudanus in 1610. On these engravings, see the forthcoming dissertation by Corrie van Maris, tentatively titled "De wisselwerking tussen kunst en wetenschap aan de Leidse universiteit in 1610," Leiden University.

13   Piet Bakker, "Gerrit Dou and His Collectors in the Golden Age" (2017), in *The Leiden Collection Catalogue*, 3rd ed., ed. Arthur K. Wheelock and Lara Yeager-Crasselt, 2020–, http://www.theleidencollection.com/essays/gerrit-dou-and-his-collectors-in-the-golden-age/.

14   See, for example, Lawrence M. Principe, *The Secrets of Alchemy* (Chicago: University of Chicago Press, 2013); and Sven Dupré, ed., *Laboratories of Art: Alchemy and Art Technology from Antiquity to the Eighteenth Century* (Berlin: Spinger, 2014).

15   H. D. Schepelern, ed., *Olai Borrichii Itinerarium 1660–1665: The Journal of the Danish Polyhistor Ole Borch* (Copenhagen: Danish Society of Language and Literature, 1983), 2: 135.

16   Theodoor Herman Lunsingh Scheurleer, C. Willemijn Fock, and A. J. van Dissel, eds. *Het Rapenburg: Geschiedenis van een Leidse gracht*, 6 vols. (Leiden: Rijksuniversiteit Leiden, 1986–92), 3: 270; Pamela H. Smith, "Science and Taste: Painting, Passions, and the New Philosophy in Seventeenth-Century Leiden" *Isis* 90 (1999): 421–61; E. J. Sluijter, "All Striving to Adorne Their Houses with Costly Pieces: Two Case Studies of Paintings in Wealthy Interiors," in *Art and Home: Dutch Interiors in the Age of Rembrandt*, exh. cat., Mariët Westermann (Denver: Denver Art Museum, 2002), 105–16; and Angela K. Ho, *Creating Distinction in Dutch Genre Painting: Repetition and Invention* (Amsterdam: Amsterdam University Press, 2017).

17   See Svetlana Alpers, *The Art of Describing: Dutch Art in the Seventeenth Century* (Chicago: University of Chicago Press, 1983).

18   G. J. Hoogewerf, *De twee reizen van Cosimo de' Medici, prins van Toscane, door de Nederlanden (1667–1669): journalen en documenten* (Amsterdam: Johannes Müller, 1919), 237, 251.

19   Smith, "Science and Taste," 423–24.

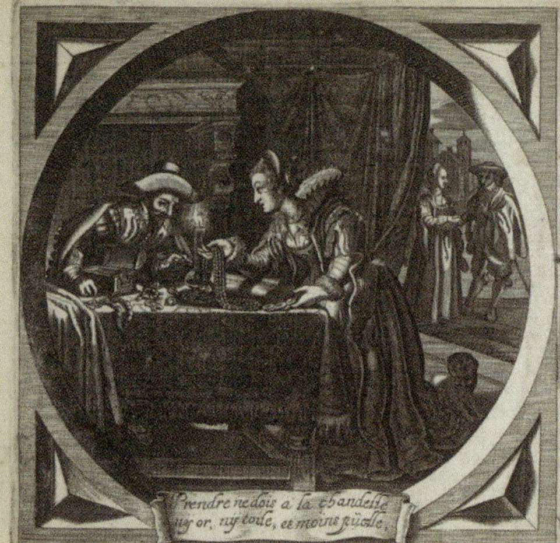

DIt wijf dat ghy hier voor u siet,
   En gelt aen desen koop-man biet;
Dit wijf is wonder slecht bedacht,
Want sy koopt peerels inder nacht,
Sy koopt in haest by 't keersen-licht,
Daer toe men houft een vol gesicht.
   Wel, Iuffer, wat ick bidden mach,
Ey, sluyt geen koop als metten dach,

Maer

Maer laet den nacht eerst over gaen,
Of wis ghy sult bedrogen staen,
Want koopt ghy niet ter rechter tijt,
Soo koopt ghy niet als enckel spijt.

   Gesellen, die des avonts vrijt,
En dickmael wonder jachtigh zijt,
En vaert niet inder haesten voort,
En spreeckt niet haest het groote woort,
En geeft voór al u troutjen niet,
Tot ghy het lief by daeghe siet:
Houdt seker dat de keerse liegt,
Houdt seker dat de nacht bedrieght,
En dat men met een korten spoet,
Noyt groote dingen wel en doet.

   'tIs waer, dat even inder nacht
Een saecke dient te zijn bedacht;
Maer al wat dienstigh is gesien
Dat moet by hellen dach geschien.

   „ Geen schoone perel dient gesocht,
„ Geen fijne webbe dient gekocht,
„ Geen vrijster oyt te zijn gemijnt,
„ Dan als de gulde sonne schijnt,
„ Want, die in duyster henen loopt,
„ En even dan juweelen koopt,
„ Of s'nachts sich koppelt aen een vrouw,
„ Die queelt by daeghe van berouw.
„ Dus wildy niet bedrogen zijn,
„ Soo wacht den klaren Sonne-schijn,
Soo wacht, ô grage vryer, wacht,
Tot dat het stuck wel is bedacht,
En ghy oock soete Vrijsters beyt
Tot alles wel is over-leyt.

D 2

Caroline Van Cauwenberge

GERRIT DOU (1613–1675)

Gerrit Dou, considered the founder of the school of Leiden *fijnschilders* (fine painters), was born in Leiden on April 7, 1613, to Marritje Jansdr van Rosenburg (d. 1657) and Douwe Jansz de Vries van Arentsvelt of Harlingen (ca. 1584–ca. 1656). Dou first received instruction in the art of glass engraving from his father, at the age of nine, and subsequently trained with the engraver Bartholomeus Willemsz Dolendo (ca. 1571–ca. 1629) and the glass painter Pieter Couwenhorn (ca. 1599–1654). After this initial period of study, Dou worked, together with his brother, Jan (1609–ca. 1647), in their father's workshop from 1625 to 1627.

In 1628, at the age of fourteen, Dou was apprenticed to Rembrandt van Rijn (1606–1669). According to the artist's first biographer, Jan Jansz Orlers (1570–1646), Dou developed into "an excellent master, especially in small, subtle, and intricate things," during his time in Rembrandt's workshop.[1] After the latter's departure to Amsterdam in 1631, Dou established himself as an independent master in Leiden and perfected his increasingly smooth and delicate style in the execution of small-scale works.

Dou specialized in genre painting, particularly domestic scenes set in interior spaces, but he also painted a wide range of subjects, including portraits, still lifes, candlelit nocturnal scenes, and history paintings, as well as—unusually—nudes. He is especially known for his trompe l'oeil niche paintings, in which one or two figures are portrayed engaged in an activity at a stone windowsill. This compositional device appears to break the pictorial threshold, creating the illusion that the figures cross into the viewer's space.

Dou was internationally celebrated for his refined technique and small-scale paintings with enamel-like surfaces. He became one of the most highly sought after—and best paid—painters in the Netherlands. His patrons included many European rulers, among them Queen Christina of Sweden (1626–1689) and King Charles II of England (1630–1685). Despite his international renown, Dou remained in Leiden throughout his career and was one of the founders of the city's Guild of St. Luke in 1648.

Dou's reputation attracted many apprentices, including Frans van Mieris (1635–1681), father of Willem van Mieris (1662–1747); Godefridus Schalcken (1643–1706); Pieter Cornelisz van Slingelandt (1640–1691); and Dominicus van Tol (ca. 1635–1676) and Jacob Toorenvliet (1640–1719), both relatives of the artist.

Dou never married. He died in Leiden in 1675 and was buried in the Pieterskerk. His enormous impact on pupils and numerous followers shaped a generation of Leiden *fijnschilders* who would continue to prosper well into the eighteenth century.

GABRIEL METSU (1629–1667)

Gabriel Metsu was born in Leiden at the end of 1629. His father, Jacques Metsu (ca. 1588–1629) was a Flemish painter and tapestry designer who died shortly before his son was born. Metsu was raised by his mother,

Prendre ne dois á la chandelle / Ny or, ny toile, et moins pucelle (Do not chose by candlelight / neither gold, nor cloth, and least of all a maiden), engraving, 5 3/16 × 5 5/16 in. (13.2 × 13.5 cm), in Jacob Cats, *Spiegel van den ouden ende nievven tijd (Mirror of Old and New Time)* (The Hague: Issac Burchoorn, 1632), 26–27. Kislak Center for Special Collections, Rare Books, and Manuscripts, University of Pennsylvania, Philadelphia.

Jacquemijn Garniers (ca. 1590–1651), a midwife, and his stepfather, Cornelis Bontecraey (d. 1649), a skipper.

There is much uncertainty regarding Metsu's early artistic training. According to Arnold Houbraken (1660–1719), the artist studied with Gerrit Dou (1613–1675), but the broad and fluid manner of Metsu's early paintings, mostly history scenes, shares little with Dou's meticulous technique as a *fijnschilder*. Instead, Metsu may have trained initially under fellow Catholic Claes Pietersz de Grebber (1590–1650), a Haarlem silversmith who had moved to Leiden in 1640, and his son, history painter Anthonie Claesz de Grebber (ca. 1622–1691). Metsu's name appears on a 1644 list of Leiden painters who acted in support of the establishment of a local Guild of St. Luke. At that time barely fifteen years old, Metsu was probably not yet active as an independent master, but he was likely already acknowledged as a talented young artist. The painters' guild in Leiden was founded shortly thereafter in 1648, and Metsu joined as one of its first members.

Metsu likely left Leiden around 1650 for a period of training and practice in Utrecht with the history painter Nicolaus Knüpfer (ca. 1603–1655). The landscape painter Jan Baptist Weenix (1621–1660/61) may also have impacted Metsu's artistic approach in these years. The two Utrecht artists introduced the young Leiden painter to large-scale works executed with broad, sweeping brushstrokes and new figural types and settings. After his brief stay in Utrecht, Metsu returned to Leiden.

In 1654, Metsu left his native city permanently to settle in Amsterdam, where he changed the thematic and stylistic approach to his art, turning away from history scenes to genre paintings. The changing art market and success of works by Gerrit Dou and other Leiden *fijnschilders* offered an important model to Metsu and may have prompted the artist's greatly refined depictions of upper-class domestic interior scenes.

In 1658, Metsu married Isabella de Wolff (1631–1718), daughter of the painter Maria de Grebber (1602–1680) and niece of Haarlem painter Pieter de Grebber (ca. 1600–1652/53). Metsu was just thirty-eight years old when he died in Amsterdam in 1667. His only known pupils are Michiel van Musscher (1645–1705) and Joost van Geel (1631–1698).

WILLEM VAN MIERIS (1662–1747)

Willem van Mieris was born in Leiden on June 3, 1662. Like his older brother, Jan (1660–1690), Van Mieris learned the art of painting from their father, Frans van Mieris the Elder (1635–1681), the renowned pupil of Gerrit Dou (1613–1675). Upon the sudden death of Frans van Mieris in 1681, Willem, only eighteen years old, took charge of the family workshop. Two years later, he joined the Leiden Guild of St. Luke, and he would later serve several terms on the guild's board. During the 1680s, together with Jacob Toorenvliet (1640–1719) and Carel de Moor (1655–1738), he cofounded the Leiden Drawing Academy, which he and De Moor directed until 1736.

Van Mieris worked in the style of the Leiden fine painters throughout his career by producing small-scale, detailed genre scenes. In addition, he copied paintings by Gerrit Dou and his father, which continued to be popular among collectors. Willem van Mieris was one of the most successful painters of his time. He never lacked commissions and was supported by a number of important patrons, including the affluent Leiden merchant Pieter de la Court van der Voort (1664–1739) and members of the foreign aristocracy, such as Duke Anton Ulrich von Braunschweig-Wolfenbüttel (1633–1714).

Van Mieris was a trusted member of Leiden's community and enjoyed high social status as well as a reputation as a learned artist. In addition to collecting a substantial number of books, he wrote about the art of painting, though none of his own texts were ever published. In 1695, Van Mieris enrolled at Leiden University.

His enrollment was not associated with a specific discipline and may have been motivated by the tax benefits it afforded.

The decline of Van Mieris's sight at the end of this life made it impossible for the painter to continue working. He died in 1747 in Leiden, where he was buried in the Pieterskerk. Van Mieris bequeathed his studio and library to his son, Frans van Mieris the Younger (1689–1763), who followed in his father's and grandfather's footsteps in painting.

PIETER CORNELISZ VAN SLINGELANDT (1640–1691)

Pieter Cornelisz van Slingelandt was born in Leiden on October 20, 1640, to Cornelis Pietersz van Slingelandt, a prosperous mason, and Trijntje van Polanen. Of their ten children, Van Slingelandt was the only one who never married. The painter probably lived with his parents until at least 1678.

During the late 1650s, Van Slingelandt was apprenticed to Gerrit Dou (1613–1675). Like his teacher, Van Slingelandt specialized in small-scale genre paintings and portraits with a meticulous and polished style. According to Arnold Houbraken (1660–1719), some of Van Slingelandt's paintings even "surpassed Dou in terms of elaboration and refinement; yet there are also some which, having received the same treatment, are somewhat stiff."[2] Van Slingelandt's laborious technique required a lot of patience, and he was known to sometimes spend years working on a painting before completing it. This painstaking method was indebted to Dou, as were Van Slingelandt's niche paintings, in which an illusionistic stone arch window ledge frames the scene.

In 1661, Van Slingelandt joined the Leiden painters' guild and established himself as an independent master with a thriving studio. His pupils included Jacob van der Sluys (1660–1732) and Jan Tilius (1653–in or after 1694).

Van Slingelandt's small, precious portraits on panel or copper were highly valued by the refined Dutch elite during his lifetime, and he was able to fetch steep prices for his paintings. His working method naturally also contributed to his high prices. However, according to Houbraken, "his time-consuming manner of working earned [him] more fame than money."[3] In 1691, Van Slingelandt was elected as dean of the Leiden Guild of St. Luke. Unfortunately, he died the same year.

DOMINICUS VAN TOL (ca. 1635–1676)

Dominicus van Tol was probably born around 1635 in Bodegraven, where his father, Simon van Tol (d. ca. 1660), was active as a public notary between 1630 and 1643. Van Tol's mother was Catharina Vechters (ca. 1602–1674), daughter of glassmaker Vechter Vechtersz van Strijtvelt (d. 1604) and half sister of the renowned Leiden fine painter Gerrit Dou (1613–1675). In 1643, the family moved to Leiden.

Because of the close ties between the Van Tol and Dou families, scholars presume that Dou served as Van Tol's first teacher. Dou's influence on Van Tol's art is also evident in terms of both subject matter and style. Van Tol often integrated Dou's motifs in his own works, such as the illusionistic device of the window sill. And while Van Tol largely executed his works with more fluid brushwork than this master, he could also emulate the virtuoso refined style of Dou. In fact, some paintings by Van Tol have even been mistakenly attributed to Dou in the past.

In 1664, Van Tol enrolled in the Leiden Guild of St. Luke and established himself as an independent master. However, the declining art market in Leiden may have motivated the artist to move to Utrecht in 1669. There, he married Maria Pollion (d. 1679) in 1670. When the French army occupied the town two years later, the couple fled, likely with their newborn son Simon Petrus (1672–1720), to Amsterdam, where their daughter Johanna Catharina was baptized in 1674.

Van Tol returned to Leiden in 1675 and again became a member of the city's painters' guild. It seems that he still did not prosper as an artist, and in 1676, his request to sell beer from his house was granted. It is uncertain whether he ever established a tavern, as he died the same year, leaving substantial debts.

JACOB TOORENVLIET (1640–1719)

Jacob Toorenvliet was born in Leiden in 1640. His first teacher was his father, Abraham Toorenvliet (1620–1692), a renowned drawing instructor and glass painter who also trained Frans van Mieris the Elder (1635–1681) and Mathijs Naiveau (1647–1726). Like Van Mieris and Naiveau, Toorenvliet continued his training with Gerrit Dou (1613–1675) in the 1650s. Dou was closely connected to the Toorenvliet family through Abraham Toorenvliet's second marriage to Geertruy Somers (d. before 1656) in 1650. Geertruy was the widow of Jan Dou (1609–ca. 1647), Gerrit's brother.

Around 1661, shortly after the completion of his artistic training, Toorenvliet embarked on a seventeen-year Grand Tour. The following year, in Vienna, he likely met the Catholic history painter Nicolaes van Roosendael (1634/35–1686), with whom he traveled to Rome. There, Toorenvliet joined the *Bentvueghels*, an artists' fraternity of Dutch and Flemish painters living in the Eternal City, and he studied the work of the great Italian masters. In 1664, Toorenvliet left Rome for Venice, where he married a wealthy woman and stayed for about three years. Around 1667, he returned to Vienna, where he likely remained until 1679, working as an artist. There, Toorenvliet executed most of his small-scale copper paintings, which depict refined genre scenes. His delicate rendering of a wide variety of textures and the minute details in his work owe much to his time with Dou.

In 1679, after the deaths of his first wife and two sons, Toorenvliet returned to Leiden and married Susanna Verhulst. The couple subsequently moved to Amsterdam, where their daughter was baptized in a clandestine Catholic church in 1680. Their son, Abraham (1682–ca. 1735), would also become a painter.

In 1686, Toorenvliet again returned to Leiden, where he joined the city's Guild of St. Luke. From 1695 to 1712, he served alternately as dean and headman of the guild. In 1694, Toorenvliet cofounded the Leiden Drawing Academy, together with Willem van Mieris (1662–1747) and Carel de Moor (1655–1738). A 1717 document lists Toorenvliet as *informator pingendi* of Leiden University, indicating that he also gave drawing lessons there. Toorenvliet died in 1719 in Oegstgeest, near Leiden, where he lived after the death of his second wife in 1713.

NOTES

[1] "Een uytnemend Meester, insonderheydt in cleyne, subtile ende curieuse dingen." Jan Jansz Orlers, *Beschrijvinge der stad Leyden* (Leiden, 1641), 377.

[2] "Die in uitvoerigheit en gepolystheit boven die van zyn Meester uitstaken; maar dit is er van dat dezelve door zulk doen wel wat styver zijn." Arnold Houbraken, *De groote schouburgh der Nederlantsche konstschilders en schilderessen* (Amsterdam, 1718–21; rev. ed., The Hague, 1753, reprint, Amsterdam, 1980), 3: 126–27.

[3] "Won [hy] door zyne tydslytende wyze van schilderen meer roem als gelt aan." Houbraken, *De groote schouburgh*, 3: 127.

Portrait of Daniel Heinsius, engraving, 6 1/16 × 4 1/16 in. (15.4 × 10.3 cm), in Johannes van Meurs, *Illustris Academia Lugd-Batava (The Illustrious Academy of Lugd-Batavia)* (Leiden: Andream Cloucquium, 1613), 209. Kislak Center for Special Collections, Rare Books, and Manuscripts, University of Pennsylvania, Philadelphia.

Filius, C. familiæ erciscundæ. | Illustratio Historiæ Mosaicæ, ex
& alias quasdam iuris par- | scriptis Ethnicorum.
tes , exercitij gratia con- | Annales belli Belgici, à digres-
scripta. | su Philippi II. Regis in His-
Item, Comparatio rerum publi- | paniam , ad Inducias usque:
carum , Atheniensis, Roma- | annorum plus quadraginta
næ veteris, & Batavica. | tempus libris viginti tribus
Notæ in Hymnos Orphei, qui di- | complexi.
cuntur.

Est in cum hoc Epigramma;

*D*Epositum cœli, quod iure Batavia mater
Horret, & haud credit se peperisse sibi,
Talem oculis, talem ore tulit se maximus Hugo;
Instar creæ hominis, cætera crede Dei.

DANIEL HEINSIVS.

DANIEL

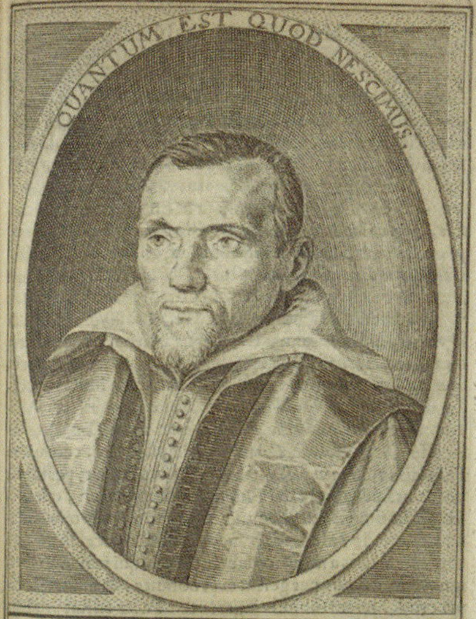

DANIEL HEINSIUS BIBLIOTHE-
CARIUS ET POLITICES PROF.

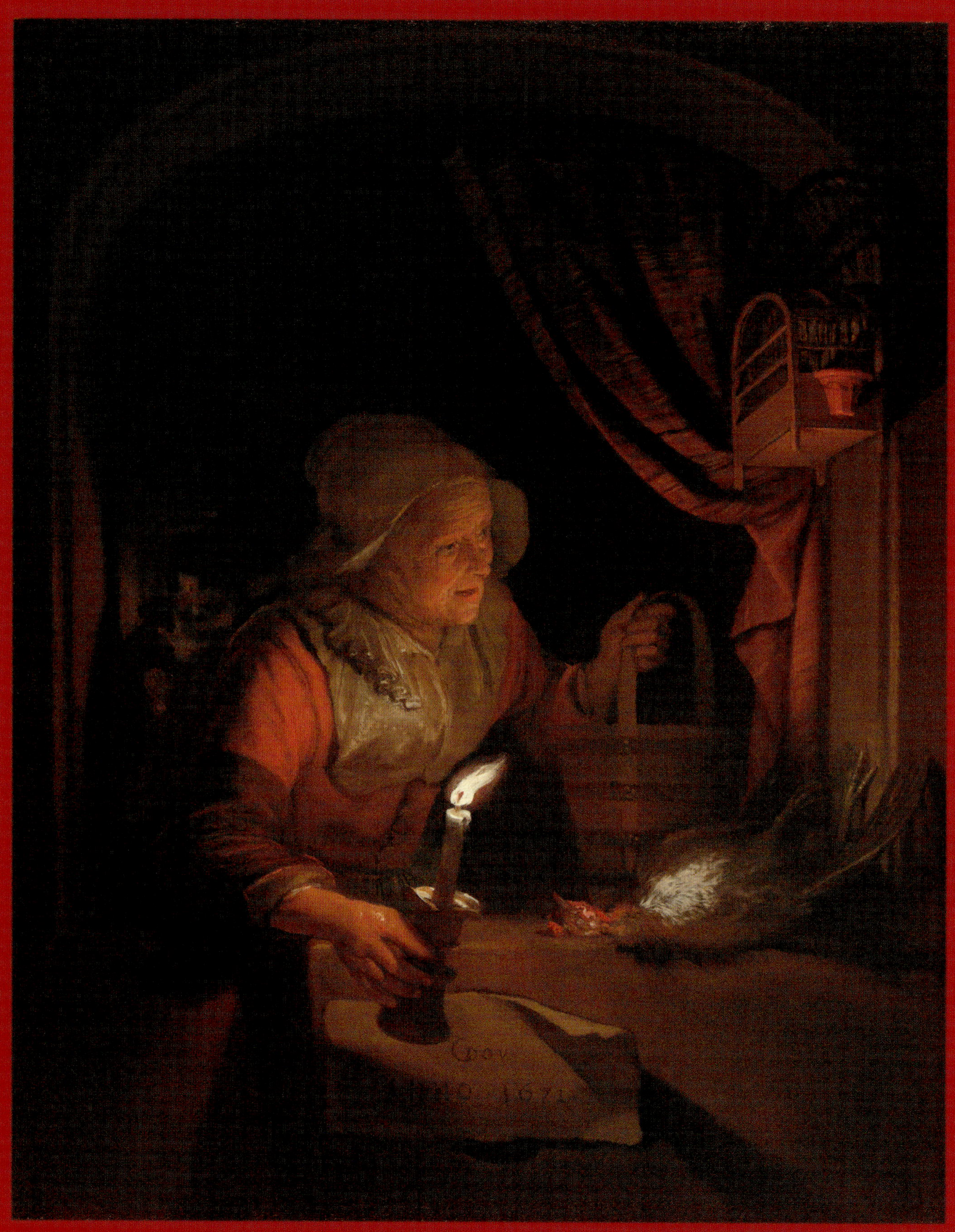

CHECKLIST OF THE EXHIBITION

PAINTINGS

GERRIT DOU (DUTCH, 1613–1675)

Girl at a Window, ca. 1655
Oil on panel
10 ⁹⁄₁₆ × 7 ½ in. (26.9 × 19 cm)
The Sterling and Francine Clark Art Institute,
Williamstown, Massachusetts, 1955.716
Cat. 1, ill. p. 8

Old Woman at a Window with a Candle, 1671
Oil on panel
Signed and dated bottom center in brown paint: "GDou /
Anno 1671"
10 ⁷⁄₁₆ × 8 ¹⁄₁₆ in. (26.5 × 20.5 cm)
The Leiden Collection, New York, GD-103
Cat. 2, ill. p. 68

GABRIEL METSU (DUTCH, 1629–1667)

Public Notary, ca. 165(3?)
Oil on panel
Inscribed and dated in light-colored paint on sign, lower left:
"openbaer Notarus / 165[3?]"
16 ⅛ × 12 ¹³⁄₁₆ in. (41 × 32.5 cm)
The Leiden Collection, New York, GM-101
Cat. 3, ill. p. 35

Woman Reading a Book by a Window, ca. 1653–54
Oil on canvas
Signed in dark paint on white letter, left of red plume: "[F?]
Gabriel/Metsu"
41 ⁵⁄₁₆ × 35 ¾ in. (105 × 90.7 cm)
The Leiden Collection, New York, GM-105
Cat. 4, ill. pp. 18 and 34

Woman Drawing Wine from a Barrel, ca. 1656–58
Oil on canvas
14 ½ × 13 ⅛ in. (36.8 × 33.3 cm)
The Leiden Collection, New York, GM-112
Cat. 5, ill. p. 74

WILLEM VAN MIERIS (DUTCH, 1662–1747)

Hermit Praying in the Wilderness, 1707
Oil on panel
Signed and indistinctly dated in dark paint, upper right corner:
"W. Van. Mieris, Fe Anº 1707"
8 ¼ × 6 ⅞ in. (21 × 17.4 cm)
The Leiden Collection, New York, WM-100
Cat. 6, ill. p. 53

PIETER CORNELISZ VAN SLINGELANDT (DUTCH, 1640–1691)

Portrait of a Man Reading a Book, 1668
Oil on copper
Signed and dated in dark paint along page edges of book:
"PSlingeland / 1668"
6 ⅜ × 5 in. (16.2 × 12.6 cm)
The Leiden Collection, New York, PvS-100
Cat. 7, ill. p. 6

DOMENICUS VAN TOL (DUTCH, ca. 1635–1676)

Children at a Window Blowing Bubbles, ca. 1660
Oil on panel
10 ⁷⁄₁₆ × 8 ¹⁄₁₆ in. (26.5 × 20.5 cm)
The Leiden Collection, New York, DT-101
Cat. 8, ill. p. 12

Boy with a Mousetrap by Candlelight, ca. 1664–65
Oil on panel
11 ¹³⁄₁₆ × 9 ³⁄₁₆ in. (30 × 23.3 cm)
The Leiden Collection, New York, DT-100
Cat. 9, ill. p. 10

JACOB TOORENVLIET (DUTCH, 1640–1719)

Alchemist, 1684
Oil on copper
Inscribed and dated in light-colored paint centered along reverse:
"Jacob Toorenvliet. fec 1684."
12 ⁷⁄₁₆ × 10 in. (31.6 × 25.3 cm)
The Leiden Collection, New York, JT-107
Cat. 10, ill. p. 58

Gerrit Dou, *Old Woman at a Window with a Candle*, 1671, oil on panel, 10 ⁷⁄₁₆ × 8 ¹⁄₁₆ in. (26.5 × 20.5 cm). The Leiden Collection, New York.

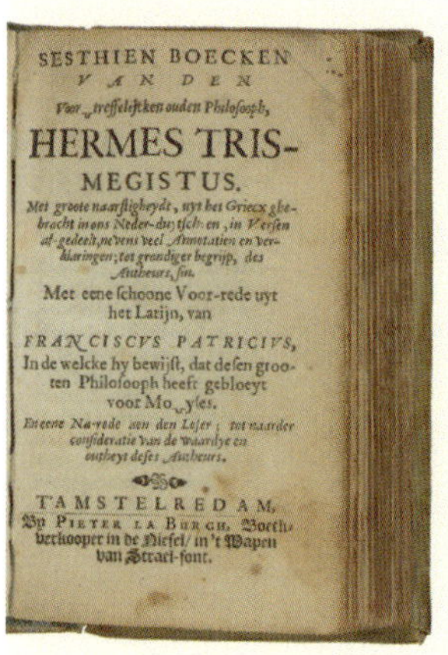

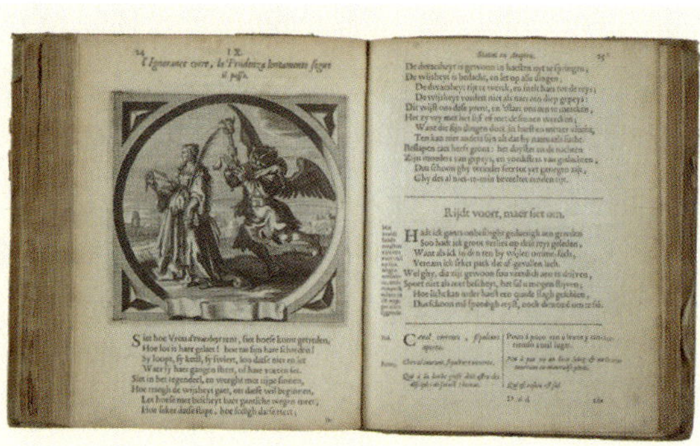

ABRAHAM WILLEMSZ VAN BEYERLAND (DUTCH, 1586/87–1648)

Sesthien Boecken van den Voor-treffelijcken ouden Philosooph, Hermes Trismegistus. Met groote naarstigheydt, uyt het Griecx ghebracht in ons Neder-duytsch; en, in Versen af-gedeelt, nevens veel Annotatien en verklaringen; tot grondiger begrijp, des Autheurs, sin Met eene schoone Voor-rede uyt het Latijn, van Franciscus Patricius, In de welcke hy bewijst, dat desen grooten Philosooph heeft gebloeyt voor Moyses. En eene Na-rede aen den Leser, tot naarder consideratie van de waardye en outheyt deses Autheurs (Sixteen Books of the Outstanding Old Philosopher, Hermes Trismegistus. With great diligence translated from Greek into our Dutch and divided in verses, in addition to many annotations and explanations, for better understanding of the authors. With a preface from Latin, by Franciscus Patricius, in which he proves that this great Philosopher has bloomed before Moses. And an Epilogue for the reader, for further consideration of the value and antiquity of these authors)

Amsterdam: Pieter la Burgh, 1652

Printed book

5 3/8 × 2 15/16 × 1 1/2 in. (13.6 × 7.5 × 3.8 cm)

Kislak Center for Special Collections, Rare Books, and Manuscripts, University of Pennsylvania, Philadelphia

Cat. 11, pictured: title page

JACOB CATS (DUTCH, 1577–1660)

Spiegel van den ouden ende nievven tijd (Mirror of Old and New Time)

The Hague: Isaac Burchoorn, 1632

Printed book with copperplate engravings

9 1/8 × 7 5/16 × 1 9/16 in. (23.2 × 18.5 × 4 cm)

Kislak Center for Special Collections, Rare Books, and Manuscripts, University of Pennsylvania, Philadelphia

Cat. 12, pictured: pp. 24–25; ill. p. 62

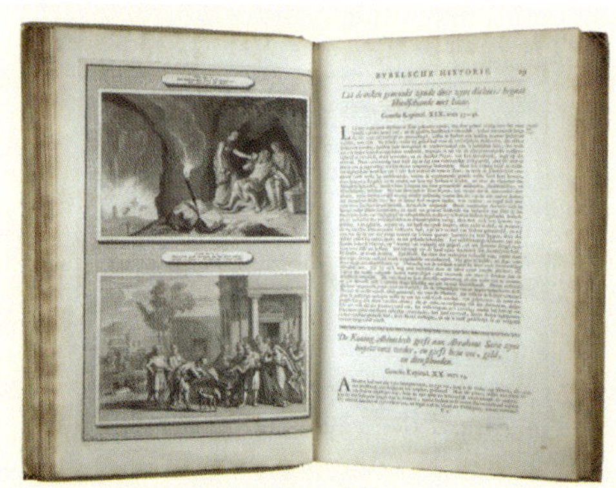

DAVID MARTIN (FRENCH, 1639–1721)

Historie des Ouden en Nieuwen Testaments: verrykt met meer dan vierhonderd printverbeeldingen in koper gesneeden (History of the Old and New Testaments, Enriched with More Than Four Hundred Printed Images Engraved in Copper)

Amsterdam: Pieter Mortier, 1700

Printed book with engravings

17 1/8 × 10 13/16 × 3 13/16 in. (43.5 × 27.5 × 9.7 cm)

Kislak Center for Special Collections, Rare Books, and Manuscripts, University of Pennsylvania, Philadelphia

Cat. 13, pictured: pp. 28–29

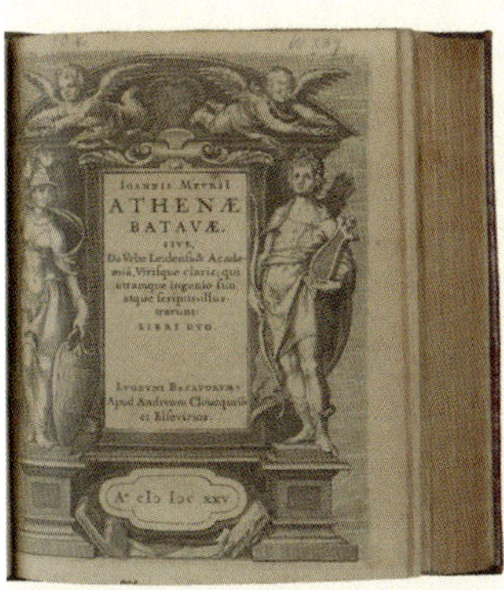

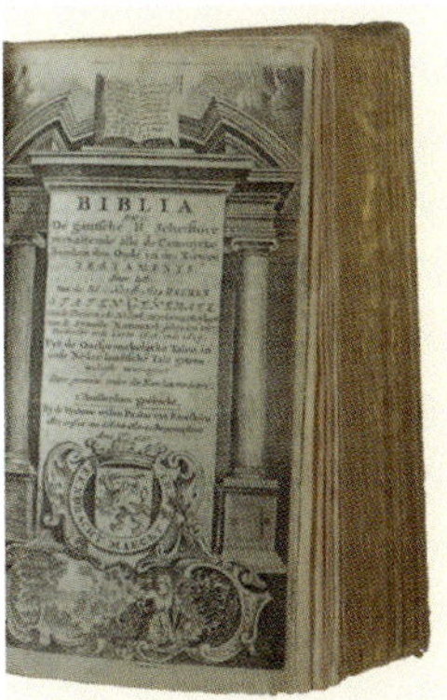

JOHANNES VAN MEURS (DUTCH, 1579–1639)

Illustris Academia Lugd-Batava: id est virorum clarissimorum icones, elogia ac vitae, qui eam scriptis suis illustrarunt (The Illustrious Academy of Lugd-Batavia: That Is, the Images, Sayings, and Lives of the Most Famous Men Who Distinguished It with Their Writings)

Leiden: Andream Cloucquium, 1613

Printed book

7 ¹¹⁄₁₆ × 6 ⅛ × 1 ⅝ in. (19.5 × 15.6 × 4.2 cm)

Kislak Center for Special Collections, Rare Books, and Manuscripts, University of Pennsylvania, Philadelphia

Cat. 14, pictured: title page; ill. pp. 14–15, p. 67

PAULUS VAN RAVESTEŸN (DUTCH, DATES UNKNOWN)

Dat is Biblia. De gantsche H. Schrifture: Vervattende alle de Canonycke Boecken des Oude[n] en des Nieuwen Testaments / door last Van de Ed. Hoogh-Mog. Heeren Staten Generael vande Vereenigde Nederl. En volgens t Besluyt van De Synode Nationael, gehouden tot Dordrecht inde Iaren 1618, ende 1619; Uyt de Oorspronckelijcke Talen in onse Neder-Landtsche Tale getrouwelijck over-geset (The Entire Holy Scripture: Including All the Canonical Books of the Old and the New Testaments / Commissioned by the noble delegates of the States General of the United Netherlands. And according to the decision of the National Synod, held in Dordrecht in the years 1618 and 1619; faithfully translated from the original languages into our Dutch language)

Amsterdam: Paulus van Ravesteŷn, 1657

Printed book in a contemporary embroidered binding, the edges gilt and gauffered

6 ³⁄₁₆ × 3 ¾ × 2 ⁹⁄₁₆ in. (15.7 × 9.5 × 6.5 cm)

Kislak Center for Special Collections, Rare Books, and Manuscripts, University of Pennsylvania, Philadelphia

Cat. 15, pictured: title page; ill. inside back cover

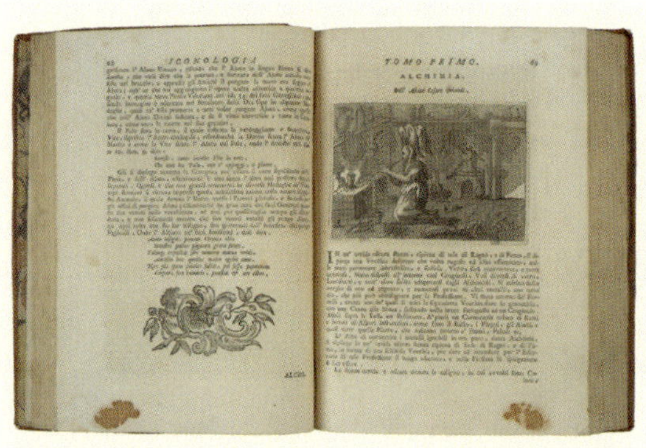

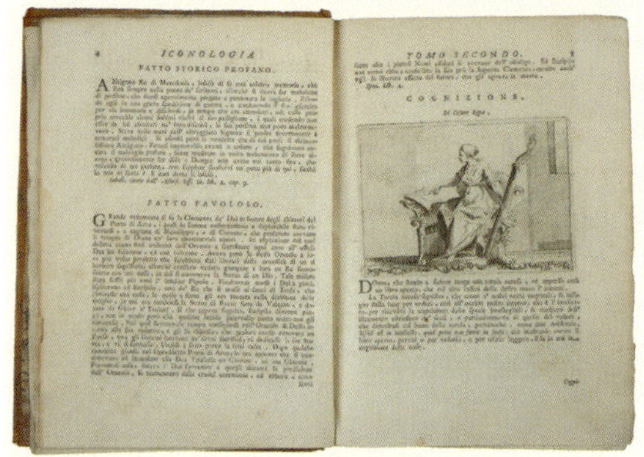

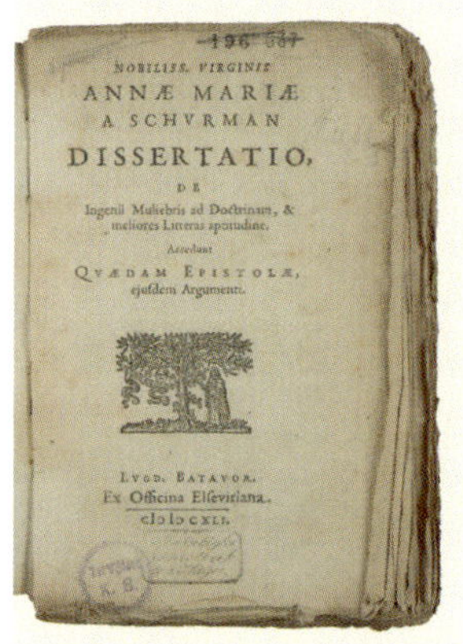

CESARE RIPA (ITALIAN, ca. 1555–ca. 1622)

Iconologia de cavaliere Cesare Ripa, Perugino (Iconologia [or Moral Emblems], of the Cavalier Cesare Ripa, Perugia), volume 1

Perugia: Piergiovanni Costantini, 1764–67

Printed book

9 ³⁄₁₆ × 7 ¼ × 1 ¾ in. (25 × 18.4 × 4.4 cm)

Kislak Center for Special Collections, Rare Books, and Manuscripts, University of Pennsylvania, Philadelphia

Cat. 16, pictured: pp. 68–69

Iconologia de cavaliere Cesare Ripa, Perugino (Iconologia [or Moral Emblems], of the Cavalier Cesare Ripa, Perugia), volume 2

Perugia: Piergiovanni Costantini, 1764–67

Printed book

10 × 7 ⁵⁄₁₆ × 1 ⅝ in. (25.4 × 18.5 × 4.2 cm)

Kislak Center for Special Collections, Rare Books, and Manuscripts, University of Pennsylvania, Philadelphia

Cat. 17, pictured: pp. 4–5

ANNA MARIA VAN SCHURMAN (DUTCH, 1607–1678)

Nobliss. virgins Annae Mariae a Schurman Dissertatio, de ingenii mulierbris ad doctrinam, & meliores litteras aptitudine: accedunt quaedam epistolae, ejusdem argumenti (The Noble Virgin Anna Maria Schurman, A Dissertation on the Suitability of a Woman's Mind for Scholarship and Literature, to Which Is Added Certain Letters, Making the Same Argument)

Lugd. Batavor: Ex Officina Elseviriana, 1641

Printed book

6 ½ × 4 ¼ × ½ in. (16.5 × 10.7 × 1.3 cm)

Kislak Center for Special Collections, Rare Books, and Manuscripts, University of Pennsylvania, Philadelphia

Cat. 18, pictured: title page

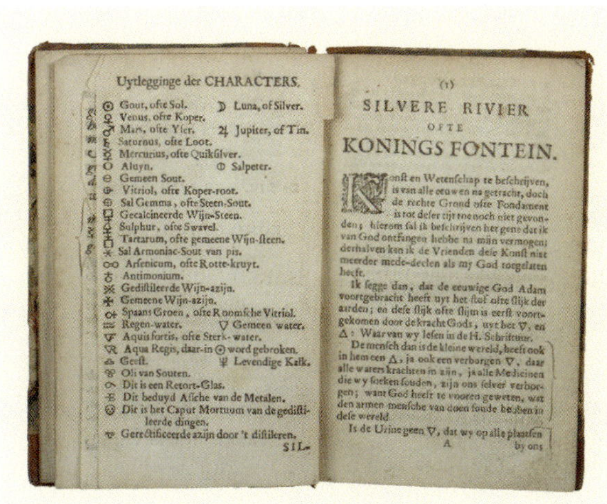

GOOSSEN VAN VREESWYK (DUTCH, 1626–ca. 1689)

Silvere Rivier, ofte, Koninsg Fontein: Waar-in ontdekt worden veele notable Medicijnen der oude Philosophen; OOK Van 't Sout en [sulphur] der Metalen, ende wat voor krachten der Medicijnen daar-in verborgen zijn; als mede het leven en de dood vande Metalen en Mineralen, haar verwen en tinctuur (Silver River, or King's Fountain: In which many notable Medicines of the old philosophers are discovered; And of the salt and [sulfur] of metals, And what kind of powers of medicine are hidden in those; As well as on the life and death of the Metals and Minerals, their paints and tinctures/extracts)

The Hague: Pieter Haaagen, 1684

Printed book

6 ⅛ × 4 ¹⁄₁₆ × 3 ⁹⁄₁₆ in. (15.6 × 10.3 × 9.1 cm)

Kislak Center for Special Collections, Rare Books, and Manuscripts, University of Pennsylvania, Philadelphia

Cat. 19, pictured: pp. iixx–1

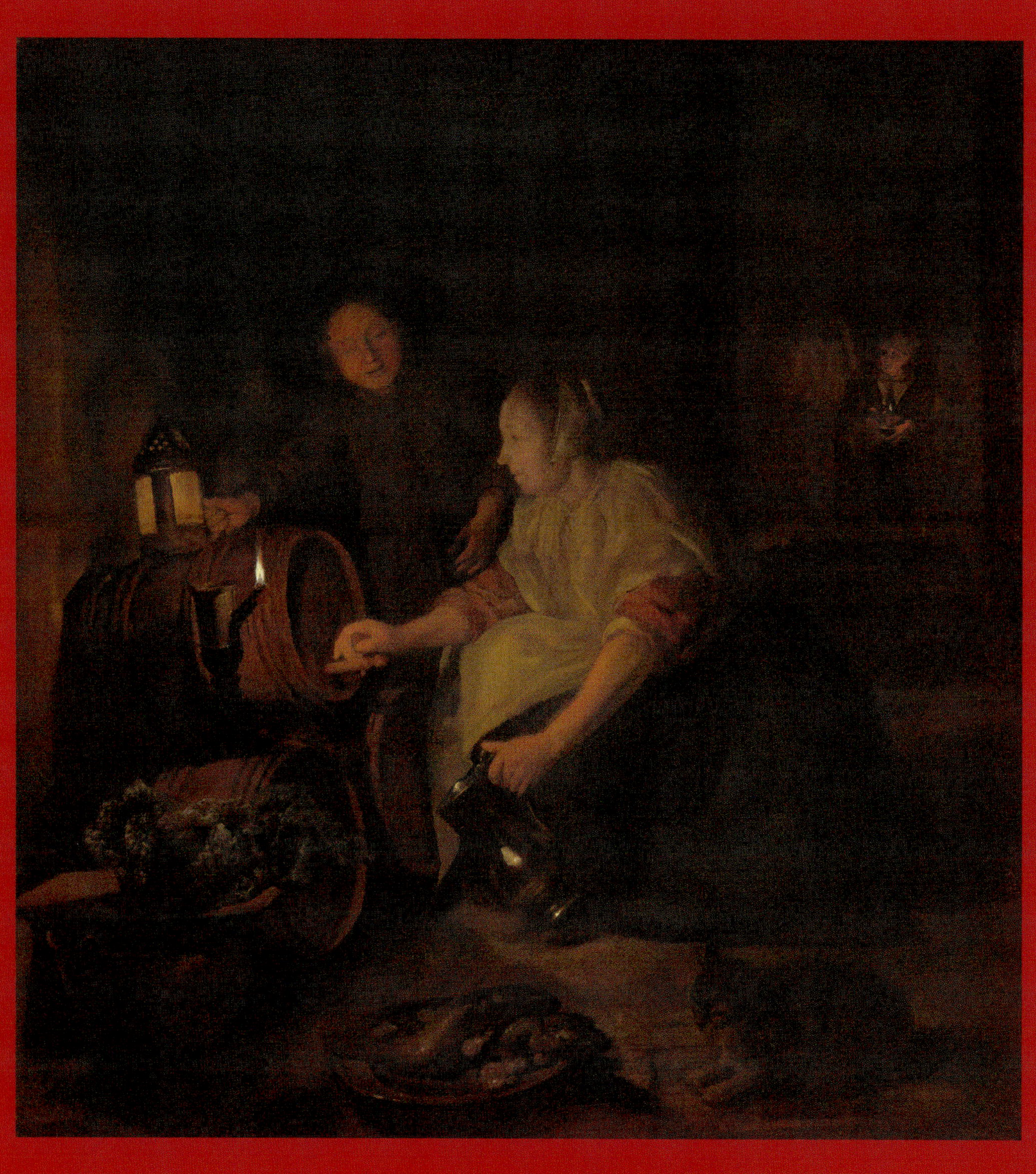

Shira Brisman is assistant professor of the history of art at the University of Pennsylvania, where she teaches early modern art. She received her BA, MA, and PhD from Yale University. Her first book, *Albrecht Dürer and the Epistolary Mode of Address* (University of Chicago Press, 2016), argues that the experience of writing, sending, and receiving letters shaped how Germany's most famous printmaker conceived of the message-bearing properties of a work of art. She is currently finishing a second monograph, titled *The Goldsmith's Debt*, which centers on the career of Christoph Jamnitzer (1563–1618) and describes the relationship between property and intellectual property at the turn of the seventeenth century. Her essays, including three prize-winning articles, have been published in journals including *Art History, Grey Room, The Journal of Medieval and Early Modern Studies, Renaissance Quarterly, Res: Journal of Anthropology and Aesthetics, Word & Image*, and the *Zeitschrift für Kunstgeschichte*.

Caroline Van Cauwenberge is the curatorial associate and digital content coordinator at The Leiden Collection, where she contributes to research on the collection and manages projects surrounding the online *Leiden Collection Catalogue*. Previously, she held positions at David Tunick, Inc., and TEFAF New York. She received her BA in art history from the KU Leuven in 2016 and her MA in art history, focusing on Netherlandish art, from the Courtauld Institute of Art in 2017.

Eric Jorink studied history and philosophy at the University of Groningen and the École des Hautes Études en Sciences Sociales in Paris. In 2004, he earned his PhD from the University of Groningen with a dissertation on science and religion, published in English as *Reading the Book of Nature in the Dutch Golden Age, 1575–1715* (Brill, 2010). He is a researcher at the Huygens Institute for Dutch History (Royal Netherlands Academy of Arts and Sciences) and Teylers Professor of Enlightenment and Religion at Leiden University. In 2012–13, he was Andrew W. Mellon Visiting Professor at the Courtauld Institute of Art, London. Jorink has published widely on the scientific culture in early modern Europe, including the culture of collecting and the relationship between visual culture and science. Together with Bart Ramakers, he edited *Art and Science in the Early Modern Low Countries* (The Netherlands Yearbook for History of Art 61, 2011).

Heather Moqtaderi is assistant director and curator of the Arthur Ross Gallery, University of Pennsylvania. She earned her MA from the Winterthur Program in Early American Culture, University of Delaware (2004). At the Arthur Ross Gallery, her most recent exhibition was *Re-materialize*, featuring contemporary works by El Anatsui, Shari Mendelson, Jackie Milad, and Alison Saar. Previous projects include the crowd-sourced exhibition *Citizen Salon* and *Landscape/ Soundscape,* which paired landscape photography from

Gabriel Metsu, *Woman Drawing Wine from a Barrel*, ca. 1656–58, oil on canvas, 14 ½ × 13 ⅛ in. (36.8 × 33.3 cm). The Leiden Collection, New York.

Penn's University Art Collection with commissioned soundscapes. Her exhibitions at other venues include *Victoriana Reimagined* at the Ebenezer Maxwell Mansion and *Duality* at the Delaware Art Museum. Moqtaderi also teaches the history of modern design as an adjunct professor at Drexel University.

Lara Yeager-Crasselt is the curator of The Leiden Collection and a specialist in seventeenth-century Dutch and Flemish art. She earned her BA from Vassar College and her PhD in art history from the University of Maryland. At The Leiden Collection, she oversees scholarly research and exhibitions, including the collection's recent global exhibition tour in China, Russia, and the United Arab Emirates, and in 2020 became co-editor of *The Leiden Collection Catalogue*. Previously, Yeager-Crasselt held positions at the Sterling and Francine Clark Art Institute, the National Gallery of Art, Washington, DC, and at KU Leuven as a Belgian American Educational Foundation fellow. Most recently, she also served as adjunct assistant professor of art at Vassar College. Yeager-Crasselt is the author of the book *Michael Sweerts (1618–1664): Shaping the Artist and the Academy in Rome and Brussels* (Brepols, 2015), as well as numerous articles on the art of the Netherlands and Italy in the early modern period.